Edward D. Moretti

MEDITATIONS ON THE SACRAMENTS

Karl Rahner

MEDITATIONS ON THE SACRAMENTS

A Crossroad Book

THE SEABURY PRESS • NEW YORK

1977 • The Seabury Press • 815 Second Avenue • New York, N.Y. 10017

Published originally under the title *Die siebenfältige Gabe*.
© 1974 by Verlag Ars Sacra Joseph Mueller, Munich. The chapters in this
book were translated and published separately in booklet form.
Copyright © 1975 by Dimension Books, Inc.

Library of Congress Cataloging in Publication Data

Rahner, Karl 1904–
Meditations on the Sacraments

Translation of Die siebenfältige Gabe.
"A Crossroad book."
1. Sacraments—Catholic Church—Meditations.
I. Title.
BX2200.R3313   234′.16   76-52938 ISBN 0-8164-0344-9

CONTENTS

PREFACE

This book brings together meditations and sermons on the seven sacraments which were written over a long period of time and under widely varying circumstances. They do not claim to be learned and documented treatises on the several sacraments, and they are not all constructed according to the same pattern. If these meditations help the reader to find a better approach to the understanding of the sacraments, I will be satisfied. I have included a sermon given at a religious profession because it seems to have the same basic theme as the meditations on marriage and priesthood, which are sacraments of one's "state in life." In so doing I am not, of course, asserting that religious profession is a sacrament.

These eight meditations are prefaced by a few thoughts about the sacraments in general. This section too is far from being a treatise on the sacraments in general, such as theological schools offer in their dogmatics courses preceding the treatises on each of the seven sacraments. But perhaps this introductory section can still be helpful in laying the groundwork for an understanding of the sacraments.

Karl Rabner

INTRODUCTION

*Preliminary Thoughts
About the Sacraments in General*

Before turning directly to the realities of faith to be found in each of the sacraments, we might benefit from some rather general considerations about the relationship between the sacraments and man as he is today (though perhaps all of us are modern in different degrees, because things do not happen to everybody at the same time everywhere). I once wrote about a "Copernican revolution" in modern man's understanding of the sacraments. Some people might consider this phrase a little too dramatic, since after all there can be no doubt that the program for this "revolution" is already laid out in the traditional understanding of our faith. Nevertheless such a revolution really is taking place—or at least it is already in the works.

What is the meaning of this "Copernican revolution" in the understanding of the sacraments, in the existential realization of the sacramental event? To make this clear we first ask ourselves: How has the average Christian up to the present day usually felt about receiving a sacrament? A descriptive answer to this question might perhaps be: both externally and internally, human life is lived in a profane world. The Christian sees this profane world, and consequently himself, as oriented toward God while remaining empirically profane. This world is put into the proper relationship to God by a mysterious quality called grace, which God keeps on giving, but (as far as it touches the world) in discrete quantities. We can know something about grace only from the outside, through verbal indoctrination; in its proper reality it is beyond our awareness—though that is how it sanctifies us, makes us pleasing to God, and unites us to him. The events in which this grace is imparted to us are called sacraments, which are sacred signs performed by the Church.

The Christian who has received a good religious education knows very well that there is such a thing as the habitual, abiding grace of justification—what the catechism calls sanctifying grace. But he usually does not apply this piece of theological knowledge to the sacraments, or, if he does, he only sees habitual grace as a prerequisite for receiving a particular sacrament. Receiving this or that sacrament is an isolated event that happens to him; it does not come from within himself. It gives him grace, but this remains as it were outside his experience of his own human existence, even though his knowledge of this sacramentally initiated grace-event, derived from sources other than his own experience, can bring about what might be called supplementary effects of consolation, of encouragement, or of impulses to do good. In my opinion, this is a pretty fair description of the traditional understanding of the sacraments.

A sacrament is thought to be a single act by which God reaches into space and time to confer grace under signs instituted by Christ. Without this grace we cannot be saved, but, because it is supernatural, it cannot be the object of "profane" awareness. Does this understanding of sacrament have any credible hold on our conscience? Does it correspond to the mentality of people today? I believe that one need have no scruple in answering both of these questions in the negative. There is another way to understand sacrament, which can be drawn from thoroughly traditional data of theology and Church teaching and which is better suited to the contemporary mentality.

"Copernican revolution" was the name we gave to the transition from the traditional concept of sacrament outlined above to the one we are now aiming at. What exactly is this new concept of sacrament? As I said, I am not thinking of some novelty, ungrounded in the traditional data of faith and theology. To that extent, it is unimportant whether we call it new or not. What I have in mind, rather, is that, if we pay attention to certain faith-insights of theology, we can understand the sacraments in a way which contrasts with the traditional understanding while remaining entirely within the bounds of orthodoxy. In order to get some preliminary idea of how this can be so, let us begin with two propositions: (1) Grace is *everywhere*, as the inmost primordial divinely implanted entelechy of world and human history. (2) Grace, in the strictest theological sense of the word, is not a particular discrete datum within consciousness—but from this it does not follow that it is a real thing beyond and outside consciousness. Instead it is the comprehensive radical opening up of man's total consciousness in the direction of the immediacy of God, an opening up that is brought about by God's own communication of Himself. Both of these propositions need a little more explanation.

Grace is everywhere as an active orientation of all created reality toward God Himself, though God does not owe it to any creature to give it this special orientation. Grace does not happen in isolated instances here and there in an otherwise profane and graceless world. It is legitimate, of course, to speak of grace-events which occur at discrete points in space and time. But then what we are really talking about is the existential and historical *acceptance* of this grace by human freedom. Grace itself, whether in the mode of merely preceding the act, or in the mode of acceptance, or in the mode of rejection, is the inmost entelechy wherever there is spirit or mind (that is, reality's openness and self-donation to God) and wherever there is transcendentality (which is radicalized by grace to orient the creature to the immediate possession of God Himself). God is the goal of the conscious world, inasmuch as He brings this movement out of the inmost center of this world to Himself. And this very radicalization of this movement of the conscious world out of its inmost center is called grace. Grace itself, therefore, is everywhere and always, even though man's freedom can sinfully say No to it, just as man's freedom can protest against man himself. This immanence of grace in the conscious world always and everywhere does not take away the gratuity of grace, because God's immediacy out of self-giving love is not something anyone can claim as his due. This immanence of grace always and everywhere does not make salvation-history cease to be history, because this history is the history of the acceptance of grace by the historical freedom of man and the history of spirit coming ever more to itself in grace.

With that I have already pretty well explained the second proposition. The world and man contain all sorts of things that can be called gifts of grace. Good weather, which puts us in a good mood, which in turn leads to a positive affective relationship towards another human being, is an example of something that can quite meaningfully be called and be experienced as grace. But when we speak of grace as such, in a strictly theological sense, and when in this sense we say that the sacraments impart grace, we mean what theology calls "sanctifying grace" or its "increase," that is, its existentially more radical acceptance. Now sanctifying grace produces created effects in man, but, without taking away from that fact, at its root it is "uncreated grace." This is God Himself imparting Himself to man so as to be both man's goal and the inmost motive force toward this goal. Without this, man could never have God as *his* goal. This grace, the inmost and inclusive movement of the spirit toward God through God even to the immediacy of God (that perfect state of human existence called the vision of God), is of its essence not an objective datum of consciousness, since it is precisely the very radicality of consciousness itself in the dynamic of knowing and in freedom. And yet it is not a reality that simply transcends consciousness.

Wherever the human being as a totality experiences himself in freedom and choice, wherever in hope he takes on an obligation which really demands more than he can give and which cannot be justified from a worldly point of view, wherever he hopes against all hope, wherever he dares to love in a way that is too costly, wherever he believes in the light although everything is dark and in meaning although everything seems to be losing its meaning, wherever he surrenders and believes this surrender to be his final victory, he experiences the radicalized transcendentality of man into the incomprehensible mystery of God. He experiences grace, even though perhaps it cannot be reflected upon and verbalized and thus made into an object of thematic conceptuality. Grace is everywhere, and it is experienced, though usually not under that name. This does not necessarily mean that every man accepts grace and thus is justified. For just as man can despair and hate himself, he can also in desperate and cowardly "modesty" deny that supreme dignity which graciously orders him to the immediacy of God and which when refused still rules him in the form of judgment.

We can now take another step. We have already said that grace is given always and everywhere and is one of the abiding existential determinants of the human spirit as it de facto exists. Nevertheless, we said, grace can and does have a history. It is the history of its being freely accepted by man and mankind, the history of man's coming to himself *as* graced and of his becoming ever more reflexly aware of it. Grace itself points us toward its goal, when it teaches us to call this process the history of revelation.

The history of the acceptance of grace can be considered here only as it occurs in individual human lives. The act of accepting the ultimate gracious dynamic toward the immediacy of God in the individual life of man is usually called a salutary act in faith, hope, and love. Human nature requires that such a salutary act always be mediated through man's taking a position toward a worldly reality (ultimately toward his neighbor). Man says his Yes or No to his graced condition (his orientation toward the immediacy of God) over some worldly reality because he has this orientation consciously and freely only in a relationship to someone or something in this world. This is why his history is the history of his free relationship to his graced transcendentality, why it is salvation-history.

And so in historical deeds and processes man's relationship to God manifests itself and becomes historically perceptible. His moral actions are the embodiment, the sign, of his ultimate relationship to God. These signs, in which the ultimate Yes or No to God's self-communication in grace is embodied and expressed, cannot of course in most cases be interpreted with any certainty *as* signs of the salutary acceptance of grace. When a person tries to reflect on them and evaluate them, they usually remain ambiguous to say the least. Not only ambiguous of themselves but also in regard to this question: Was whatever definite orientation they do have toward God also actually intended by the person who performed them? Now such moral actions do not necessarily have to have an explicitly religious thematic. As embodiment and historical perceptibility and symbolization of the acceptance of grace, they can also occur in a situation in which, without an expressly religious thematic, man's freedom unconditionally obeys the absolute dictate of conscience and so, unthematically and without reflection, affirms and accepts what we call God and the radical liberation of man in the direction of God himself through His grace.

This point will permit us to reach an understanding of the principles of what we call Christian sacraments only if we pay attention to two more things. Human actions always occur in the realm of interpersonality, they always make a difference in human relations, they always imply a communication made to others, and the interpersonal and social situation in which a person lives and deals always contributes to the shape his actions take. In Christ Jesus, the Crucified and Risen One, it has become manifest in an historically perceptible way that what has always and everywhere been brought about by grace—the salvation-history of mankind as a whole—in spite of its ambivalence between salvation and eternal perdition necessitated by man's freedom, has entered into a stage in which this history, as the history of mankind as a whole, can no longer fall short of its goal—a goal which will be achieved infallibly but without detriment to the freedom of the individual participants in this salvation-history of humanity. That is why Jesus Christ is called the primordial sacrament of salvation. By this word we mean precisely that historical event in which, as in an historical sign, God's will to save men, which triumphantly succeeds in its purpose in spite of all the sins of men and which from the beginning was implanted in the world as grace, brings about its own unmistakable historical manifestation and establishes itself in the world and not just in the transcendent will of God. The Church, as the socially constituted presence of Christ in every age up to the end, can therefore rightly be called the basic sacrament of the salvation of mankind. By this we mean that it is the sign which perpetuates Christ's presence in the world, the permanent and unsurpassable sign that the gracious entelechy of the whole of history, which brings this history into God Himself, will really be victorious in the world despite all sin and darkness and will really prevail by bringing about the completion of the world in the form of salvation rather than judgment.

Now I think we can arrive at a basic understanding of the sacraments, even though our treatment of it must unfortunately be brief. When the Church as the basic sacrament, in situations of human life which are decisive for the individual or for the group, pledges itself to man with an absolute commitment of its being *as* the basic sacrament of salvation, and does so historically and palpably, that is, in word and deed, and when man in turn accepts this the Church's pledge of salvation and acts it out as the manifestation of the acceptance of his interior grace-dynamic, then we have what we mean by the sacraments of the Church. This general description of the essence of the sacraments cannot be elucidated further in this introduction. We must forego applying it to the several sacraments of the Church and showing how it leads to an historically correct understanding of the Church's teaching that Jesus instituted the sacraments and by so doing conferred on them their power to give grace.

The reflections which we are going to make on the Eucharist, however, require that we emphasize or re-emphasize two points. First, the starting-point we took gives intelligibility to what we called the Copernican revolution in our way of looking at the sacraments. To say it once again, the sacraments are the historical manifestations of the grace which is always and everywhere at work in the world. In so far as they participate in the primordial sacrament Christ and in the basic sacrament Church, they are without doubt historical manifestations of grace which have a special character and thus differ from those always ambivalent manifestations of grace which are found in every good moral act. It is this difference, incidentally, which could be the basis for an explanation of the notion of *opus operatum*. None of this, however, alters the basic fact that the sacraments must be seen in the first place as ecclesial manifestations and historical incarnations of *that* grace which is at work everywhere in the history of mankind and manifests itself historically, though in highly diversified ways, wherever men are doing good and thereby in some inexpressible way striving for God Himself in faith, hope, and love. What we see in the sacraments, therefore, is precisely the inmost being of the history of mankind in the world inasmuch as history's inmost entelechy, by being God Himself, makes history the history of God Himself.

Secondly, when we say that the most basic thing about the sacraments is that they are signs, and if, with all their historical relativity, the sacraments are ultimately signs which grace creates for itself out of its own most distinctive essence, we are not denying that these signs are *efficacious* signs. We do not think of them as mere supplementary statements expressing a reality which exists and comes to the fullness of its being just as well without such expressions. Grace is the incarnational grace of Christ, which by its nature aims at being flesh and history. By its own inner power it creates man's acceptance. As accepted it makes itself present in the world precisely by effecting its historically perceptible acceptance in the sacraments. And so one can quite well say that the sign is the *cause* of what it signifies just as conversely it is the *effect* of what is signified. What really matters here is this simple insight: a real understanding of the Eucharist lets us see it as the manifestation of that mysterious grace which inconspicuously governs our whole life, the celebration in the community of the Church of that which wills to find its victory in the monotony and pain of daily life.

Translated by James M. Quigley, S.J.

MEDITATIONS
ON THE SACRAMENTS

1

BAPTISM

God Loves This Child

We have come together for a baptism. The child, to whom at this moment a most important thing is happening, knows nothing about it, or at least this is what we must assume. In any case he is still oblivious of what here takes a visible form in human actions and words, although we cannot know with equal certainty whether in the unfathomable depths of his soul (and we cannot say when he was first endowed with this) the light of grace may even now be burning so brightly that, although unutterable and invisible, it may already be illuminating his whole being. But in any case we are not here concerned with this.

The real and distinguishing characteristic of this sacrament is that here God is dealing with a human being. When an adult has become aware of his freedom and has taken hold of himself and his own destiny and is freely directing his life, then God speaks to him as to a colleague or a partner. There is a free, loving intercourse between God and the soul. God speaks to it in order to be answered; yet it is He who inspires the answer. He is always near to us when we listen to Him and love Him, and all our doings are inspired by Him. But it is always He who speaks the first word. Everywhere and on every occasion when a man meets his God he finds Him because God has first sought him. A man's actions are always the fruit of the free activity of God within him. For God is truly God, the supreme and sovereign grace which we can neither understand nor deserve, and which always anticipates our needs.

Since this is so, a child too can be baptized. Because he is underage and incapable of directing his life, God deals directly with him. And because He always forestalls our needs, the distance in time between His mighty lifegiving Word and our living response to it is of no significance.

What happens in the baptism of a child? Simply, what is always happening for our salvation is here more clearly revealed: God anticipates our need, His mercy enfolds us before we call upon it. He has already visited us so that we may knock on His door. He has already found us so that we may seek Him. So God already acts within this child in order that, once he has become aware of his own spiritual being, and aware of love, God may already be there as the heaven which arches over this dawn of a new life.

But what does God do to this child through the sacrament of the church, so that later on he may act for himself? What is it that God gives him here in baptism? What is done here as a sign and manifestation on the surface of life in order to express the hidden action of God is known to us all. It is the baptism, the washing of a human being with the precious water, by the power of the Word which consecrates this life to the Father and the Son and the Holy Ghost. But what is God doing under these outward signs?

This is not so easily described. Not only because God's personal love is the act of an infinite unimaginable Supreme Being and thus must necessarily remain a mystery, and we can only show we have begun to understand it when we say that it is something inexpressible and unutterable; but there is another reason too: God loves this child that is here baptized, but not just from the moment of his baptism. It is because He already loved him that the child, through God's merciful providence, comes to be baptized as the child of a Christian family. God has loved him from eternity. He has borne him in His mind from everlasting to everlasting. There was never a moment, while God lived and thought and loved, when this life, this person, and his eternal destiny were not present to Him, enfolded in His all-creative wisdom and embraced in His divine love. From all eternity He has seen this child as someone belonging to His eternal Word, the logos. For God, speaking through His eternal Word, entered what was mortal, null and void. He spent Himself as love, which He is, for the sake of that which cannot in its own right claim such a love. He gave Himself away. That is the fundamental purpose of God, the reason for all His outpourings of Himself, for the Word which becomes flesh, the divine Word which resounds with a man's voice in the dumb wilderness of mortality.

It is because of this divine Will that there are other human beings, that there is this little human being here today. He was from the first seen and desired as a brother of the Word of God become man, as one who is here for that very reason, so that God may embrace him with brotherly love in this sacrament at which He is present to give Himself away. This child has always been enfolded in God's love, has already been eagerly welcomed by Him.

In spite of the inherited guilt of original sin in which this child was born, God's love has always awaited him and included him in the divine plan of salvation. Thus God will confront him with the demands of His infinite love as soon as he has awakened to a sense of responsibility for himself, and He will offer him all His own glory as eternal life. If this be true, then it is not so easy to describe what has taken place here, since the beginning of this life was already sanctified by the saving will of God, which would in any case have sought out this human being during his life, for eternal salvation or judgment.

But as soon as we raise these questions, we are already near to grasping a blessed certainty which has its own significance in the proper understanding of baptism. Just because the glory of the divine Word enlightens every man, just because God wills that all men shall be saved and come to a knowledge of the truth, just because God does not measure out His gifts, we can believe that here, where the grace of God is invoked over this child, our appeal does not remain unheard but is accepted and answered. Here in very truth we call upon God who is gracious and merciful, wise and kind. Through His Son, with his Cross and Resurrection, He has told us that He will be to us a compassionate Father and the God of all consolation. He has shown us that even when we were sinners He loved us and in His own divine life entered the darkness of our existence, never more to depart. And therefore we have confidence in the power of the God of mercy over all the dark destinies of men from the beginning to the end. Therefore we also know that if through His Word and at His bidding His power is invoked over a human life, if we pray to the Father of mercy and to the Son who took upon Himself our mortal nature in order to redeem it, if we invoke the Holy Spirit who sanctifies and renews all things and is God's own gift of Himself to men, then there comes to pass what the words say, and what is here described truly takes place.

This does not mean that in a life so blessed there is no need for any more divine grace because it is already included in God's gracious purpose. God wants this life to be lived in time, in history. This element of time, this history which unfolds itself, is not merely the external appearance which conceals what is timeless and changeless. It is God's own history and God's own time, the divine history of salvation and mercy which must unfold here and now. It begins, grows, ripens and perfects itself in an eternity which is not only infinite truth but also the actual fruit of time and history. Therefore it cannot be that everything has already been given by God to this child, before he begins to live in time. God Himself enters into this time and acts in it just as His Son moved about in earthly time and earthly space under the infinite heaven: He was born of a woman and died under Pontius Pilate.

Certainly God was here before the beginning of time and had already embraced in His love all that was to be included in time. It would perhaps be hard to say in every case which particular fleeting moments showed God at work. But we know that His story is told in time, and therefore we can truly dare to describe what happens in this moment when a child is baptized.

It is fairly easy to describe. If we consider only the history of the child in time, then we must not anticipate any particular moment, for every moment has its own place and, in that place, all which must occur in it. But when we consider his spiritual history, then it is not true that the moment which is now here will pass away forever. Just as, when a man is begotten, a destiny begins that will never come to an end, so every moment of the history of a spiritual person is indeed the beginning of an eternity which is preserved and enshrined in every future moment, like its secret essence.

Therefore we may confidently speak of baptism and of what it does. What happens is manifest here and now. And if it is manifest, then at least we may say that what has already begun will continue to grow.

When an adult is baptized he is already what he would have become through baptism, a believer, and he is already sanctified and justified by the power of the Holy Spirit. Nevertheless, in his case too, baptism is no empty ceremony. What had already begun is now established in his riper years and, growing through time and eternity, in its own newly won eternity, will reveal itself under the signs and shadows which veil our life. It will strike deeper roots into the depths of a man's soul and penetrate more profoundly all the strata of human life, so that it is just as meaningful to baptize a man who already believes and loves as it is to baptize a child still at the start of his spiritual life.

We may now ask once more, rather impatiently: "But what *happens* in baptism?" Seen in its external aspect it is primarily an act of the Church. She baptizes through Her representative, the priest. Baptism is the gateway into the Church.

Whenever this sacrament is not invalidated by the stubborn unbelief of the person baptized (and this could never be the case where a child is concerned), baptism is the act by which a human being joins the visible company of the members of the Church of Jesus, the Church of those who acknowledge Jesus Christ, crucified and restored to life and, in serving the one living God who has revealed Himself in one Lord, seek to find perfection in the Second Coming of Christ. This child, once baptized, belongs to the one Apostolic, Catholic and Roman Church. He need not be asked whether he wishes to join the Church or not. He was not asked whether he wished to be born a human creature and to enter this mysterious life. The divine gift is always in this way freely bestowed upon him, and later he himself will have to decide what to do about it.

As God has called all to join His Church, and as She is the Ark of salvation and the blessed community of the redeemed, and as in any case She presents an unavoidable challenge to every man (even when he is not explicitly aware of Her), there is nothing wrong or arbitrary about the Church's action when, as God's emissary and speaking by His authority, She intervenes in the dawn of a human life with the announcement, proclaimed in human words, that the holy God and Creator of us all will judge us all. Our consent is not asked for what happens to us (nor are we debarred from giving this consent) any more than our consent is required for our human birth, which is given to us unasked for and which nevertheless must be accepted for good or, in spite of our unending protests, for ill. A human being becomes a member of the Church through baptism.

But this Church is the holy Church of God. She is the historical expression of God's saving purpose, the incarnation of His grace, because She is the continuation of the historical, tangible presence of the Word of God made flesh in this world. And through this membership in the Church of Christ, provided that he does not inwardly reject it, a man receives his share of the Holy Spirit of the Church, a share in Christ, in grace and righteousness. Although membership of the Church may be forfeited through unbelief and schism, baptism itself is not thereby wiped out and lost. The man remains bound to the Church; he still retains his membership in the everlasting community of the Lord. This permanent spiritual seal is therefore also his everlasting spiritual title to share in the Holy Spirit of the Church and in the grace and righteousness bestowed upon him at his baptism.

We call this sublime gift, which God bestows upon us in the rite of baptism, His sanctifying grace. But we ought to try to come to a clearer understanding of what is meant by this.

Let us now consider this mystery of our faith and of our life from a point of view which seems to present fewer difficulties. We are a mystery to ourselves. We have no abiding city. All that we do, suffer and achieve is forever merely provisional and temporary. The light around us grows ever dimmer as we move forward into infinite darkness. We are creatures who can never belong anywhere, but must always be wandering. Our quest is endless; every new certainty and every new experience drives us to ask new questions and set ourselves new tasks. We are insatiable, infinite—but ours is not the infinitude of perfection and blessed possession but the infinitude of potentialities, of ambitions and of nostalgia. If the last door in this endless nostalgic quest for what is far away were ever finally bolted and barred (and this could only happen through our own fault), then we should be condemned to all that is finite and mortal: we should be eternally lost. But now we are still pilgrims with infinity before us—we are still infinite beings. Shall we ever arrive? Shall we ever find perfection? Will the twilight ever yield to the dawn of eternal day?

7

Since we have known only finite satisfaction, which is really no satisfaction at all, we are afraid that perfection and fulfillment, the goal and the future, must prove disillusionments—and that there can be nothing to give us eternal satisfaction and blessed perfection. But because we know that all this ceaseless wandering cannot end in a void, because we believe that all longing lives by the promise of a truth, and no darkness or void could be seen and recognized as such if somewhere there were not never-ending light and infinite perfection, we are still unappeased and unsatisfied, and we still have to say of ourselves: we are infinite potentialities because we are called to an infinite perfection. How this perfection, without which we should be meaningless, will be achieved we cannot know of ourselves. We must learn it from the message of the Gospel of Christ which teaches us a twofold truth: this fulfillment is the boundless love of God Himself, which is shared with us and through which we are born again. It makes us sons and heirs with His Son, and pours the Spirit of God into our hearts, thus enabling us to share in the divine nature. And this perfection is not merely a verbal promise which must find its fulfillment in the future. The fulfillment is already here, but still hidden, believed in but not yet enjoyed. The future is already here, the life of God is already within us, the Holy Spirit is already poured out upon us, and we are already sons of God, so that now we need only to receive the revelation of what we already are. And this fulfillment of our infinite longing comes with the life of God Himself, already given to us, although it is known only to faith. We call it saving grace.

And here and now the child is given this grace because he is received into the Church, the holy community of the saved and sanctified, and is in very truth, henceforth and forever, more than a child of nature. He begins his life in such a way that when it comes to an end it may flow back into the infinity of God. He already has a life into which God's own glory has entered, he prolongs in time the life of the Father's Son, and

8

he already enjoys a foretaste of the eternal glory in which he now has a right to share. His spirit already silently yearns for his beloved Father, the strength of God is already in him, waiting to show throughout his whole life that it finds its fulfillment in the weakness of men.

Of such a life it could already be said: "I no longer live, but Christ lives in me." Here there already exists what will be revealed in a long, human life, full of blessed joy and bitter sorrow: the mystery of God, which is love. Indeed all these words, because they are human and bear the mark of this poor finite world, sound overstrained and insipid. If we choose plain and simple words they sound like comfortable platitudes. If we scrape together grand, forceful words, they sound like the clapper of a bell which is rung too loudly, shrill and violent. So we must hear them and then, as it were, forget them, and listen within ourselves to the silence of unutterable longing and let the mysterious truth speak from the depths of our heart. Then it will be as if we stood before an abyss: no plumb line can measure its depth, no sound break its silence, nothing we conceive of can fill its void, only the unfathomable mystery of man. But this abyss is already, without any outcry, without any force or violence, softly and gently filled with the immeasurable love of God. One mystery calls to the other, the mystery of man to the mystery of God, and God's mystery to man's. Both may be understood in their inconceivable essential reality and blessed power only by the man who dares to accept the burden of his own mystery as an excruciatingly painful enigma. If he believes that this all-embracing, invisible, immeasurable and unutterable mystery is sacred, and silently accepts it and yields himself lovingly to it, then he knows all. Then he understands what we mean when we say that in baptism God's own infinity enters into the mystery of man, bringing him grace and fulfillment, and he begins to go forward into the great depths of his own existence.

But what have we others to do on this occasion, when something happens between God and another human being?

Have we others also a part to play in what is taking place between heaven and earth?

We love this child, each of us in his own way and for his own reasons. And so we rejoice and are thankful for what he has received. In this moment, although he is still unaware of it, he is given the divine power to begin his endless journey to God, but this does not mean he is taken away from us. In fact, he has come even closer to our love. The shortest way to all that is unique and inalienable in another human being whom we love is the way through God. Although this may seem endless, it is not a roundabout way but the shortest of all, in fact, the only way.

How often we have found that we have grown distant from one another, or at least seem to be distant, when we love each other and wish to be nearer. Suddenly there seems to stretch between us and our fellows a strange boundless expanse, a desert in which all understanding and intimacy have become impossible. We no longer possess or understand each other: we have become strangers. We want to love our fellow men just as they are; we do not seek to fashion them arbitrarily according to our own image and likeness; we are willing humbly to leave them to develop in their own way. Yet it seems we have to choose between a closeness which tends to assimilate the lover to the loved, so that one becomes a tyrannical and despotic lawgiver to the other, or a distance which allows the other room for free growth but removes him so far from us that our love and our power to cherish him wither away.

And even if we have the silent strength and courage to leave the other alone so that he may become his real self, we must not thereby become like cold, wise, detached monads, which in unending isolation continue to circle around themselves in order that the others may be free to do the same. In this conflict of life there are many intermediate solutions prompted by affection, patience, forbearance and loving, unembittered resignation. But a final solution of this conflict can be found only in God. If God Himself, in the infinite

creative power of His love which desires to preserve the mul-
tiformity of all in one unity, is the providential distance in
which we may yet find each other, then closeness will not
produce uniformity and distance will no longer be deadly.
God Himself is that power in love which allows the loved one
freely to develop his own personality but does not break the
union between the lover and the loved. God wants us to love
everyone for what he truly is, for himself.

In union with God a man can lovingly bear his fellow man
in his innermost heart, where God is working for his everlasting salvation. For God loves men and is united with them, and
in His great mercy inspires all their good resolutions.

In baptism He says that He will also be the infinite space
around love, the space in which we can love this child and be
loved by him forevermore. So we see that when we attend a
baptism something happens in our own lives too. It establishes a spacious intimacy between us and the child.

This child is our brother. He is the son of his parents and
a brother, or at least a close relative, of the others who have
gathered to celebrate the consecration of his life to God. But
this means that we all have some share of responsibility for
him. It may one day happen that God will ask us, regarding
this child: "Cain, where is your brother, Abel?" This living
person is a part of our responsibility before God, a part of our
own life's task and so of our eternal destiny.

Shall we do our duty by him, or be blameworthy where he
is concerned? Guilty or greatly blessed, for him and for ourselves, because of the way we live, the way we speak, the
example we offer, the way we give or deny love or help when
he asks us for it? It is a dreadful mystery that every one of us
should be responsible for the fall or the resurrection of our
fellow men, for mercy or for judgment, for edification or for
scandal. And the newly baptized who enters our life in this
way, without asking our permission, is a child full of grace,
a human being with whom God united Himself when He
sent him His Holy Spirit.

The Word, when He became man, took upon Himself a

human destiny, although He was the infinite, blessed, inviolable God Himself, and if every man forms part of the destiny of this Son of Man who is God's Word, then we too shall be part of the destiny of the Word of God Himself, not only through what we are ourselves but also through what we are to this child. Here is a brother of Jesus, here is one of the little ones whom He blessed, whose persecutors He threatened with eternal damnation, because in very truth He Himself is offended when we do not behave as we should to such a child. But because God by the grace of baptism has united Himself to this child, then this ceremony holds for us too a divine promise that He will be our strength and help, so that we may worthily bear the responsibility we all share for this young life. So in the sacrament of baptism God has a word of comfort for us too: "Because I Myself in My divine power share the burden which a human being lays upon every other, so, if only you will believe, this burden will become an overflowing source of grace." Thus we also receive grace and salvation from this sacrament.

A sacrament is always a liturgical act of the Church, and every sacrament is administered by Her. The sacramental formula is Her Word, and as She is the Bride of Christ it is the Word of Christ Himself, and therefore powerful and effective, giving what it promises. But since the Church administers every sacrament, She also assumes a visible form in all those persons here present.

First of all there is the priest who baptizes. He is the agent through whom the baptism takes place, as he alone must do the ritual washing and speak the word of salvation. But if many people are gathered together, he is not alone in celebrating the baptism. Others too are truly taking part in this holy ceremony; they are gathered here as members of the Church here made visible. This is understandable insofar as the godparents are concerned. Their presence at the ceremony of baptism is required by the Church. The Church's responsibility and duty regarding the child's upbringing truly rest with them, although of course not exclusively. They promise that the child shall be brought up as a Christian. But a person may assume such an obligation only by sharing in the care and responsibility of the Church. So She is acting also through the godparents, because they represent Her and share in Her work.

In the ancient Church, at the baptism of adults, the godparents were first and foremost the witnesses of the baptism; they had to report to the bishop that the candidates were already truly in thought and deed what they were now to become sacramentally, that is, Christians. Today the godparents must, to the best of their ability, cooperate with the parents, so that they may one day testify that the Christian life which began here today through God's grace is truly manifest in this child's thoughts and actions. At the end of this new life they will only be able to assert that it continued as it began today if they too, throughout their lives, have been witnesses to Christ. In any case, the godparents appear here as sharers in the Church's responsibility and pastoral love at the dawn of this life, and so they fully participate in this sacramental rite as Her representative.

The same, though perhaps in a less obvious sense, is true of all who come to celebrate this baptism. The responsibility we bear for all our fellows, and also for this child, is not merely an individual concern of ours. We bear this responsibility as members of the Church. We should be sinning against the Church if we sinned against such a life. Here a person is baptized, here a new life is received into the life of the Church, another page of Her history is begun. For the Church is no abstract idea, but the community of all who are baptized and, in the knowledge of the true faith, received into the flock of Christ. She is not merely an official organization, for we all help to build Her, and contribute to Her life, to Her holiness, Her guilt and Her failure in history—we all bear witness to the victory of the grace of Christ, and to our weakness. So when we attend a baptism we do not go merely to see a spectacle, like the crowd waiting outside a Registry Office, waiting to stare at the bride and groom. We are gathered around the newly baptized as fellow members of the Church. We say to him: "Now you belong to us, and we to you, in quite a new way." We all have our own lives, our own responsibility—we all belong to the one Body of Christ, in whom alone we are blessed. So we all bear witness to the Church and represent Her whenever we assume a Christian responsibility for the love and care of souls. Therefore, the fact that we come to this baptism shows that we think about it in a Christian way. What happens here is an incarnation of what we have already received in our souls, and while we share in this sacramental celebration, the fruit of the Holy Spirit to which we thus bear witness ripens within us.

Last but not least, the reason why we too have a share in this celebration is because our own baptism has not yet ended. What occurred sacramentally and irrevocably, once and for all, was to last a whole life, to last for life and death; through baptism we became Christians in order to remain Christian in life and in death. When we attend another's baptism we must celebrate a renewal of our own. When we were baptized we were almost unaware of what was happening to us. We understood nothing of the worth and meaning of the sacrament. But God Himself worked in us, and that was what mattered. But ever since then we must play our part as persons, free, consenting and obedient. We now know more and more about it. For the baptism which we received was not given to us as something which was to pass away with the occasion, but as something which was to remain with us. It is always here in the present: it is not a thing of the past. It is still with us in our unalterable state as baptized people: it is the indissoluble seal which was impressed upon us. We must always keep in step with this reality, for we are far from perfect. We must be more and more on the alert, so that we may give our full and unconditional consent to what we have become. The godparent, as the child's representative, says, "I desire to be baptized," and we can always express this desire about ourselves and our own lives. As the apostle said to his disciples who asked to be ordained by the laying on of hands, "Awake to new life through the gift of grace which is bestowed upon you by the laying on of hands," so we can with almost greater right say this about the other and most fundamental sacrament, baptism, which sets upon us an unbreakable seal.

We can newly kindle this gift of grace, like a fire under the ashes of our daily lives. We can let a new, more sublime, more vigorous life grow out of the roots implanted in us by our baptism. On this day we can see ourselves in this child and in his destiny and say to ourselves: "You too began your life in this way. Did you continue so? Has the promise of this day been fulfilled in you? Has this day's sowing produced a harvest?"

The day of our baptism returns to us out of a remote past. It has returned as our future—for blessedness or for judgment. We must go forward along the way we started, we must not swerve from it as we grow older. Therefore on such a day, in such an hour, we must say within our hearts: "I desire this baptism which gives me eternal life; I repeat and promise that I will wear my wedding garment unstained all my life; the light of faith and love shall not be spent; I will go on to the end of the way which I began to follow in that day: it leads to eternal life."

We have said enough. May God say His own Word to this child, the Word of His love, His grace and His eternal faithfulness. He is faithful who begins the good work in this child —He will bring it to perfection. We will let God say His Word. May the life of this child, and our own lives also, be our answer, through God's grace.
Amen.

Translated by Dorothy White

2

CONFIRMATION

A New Baptism in the Spirit

The sacrament of confirmation does not really play an important part in the life of the average Catholic Christian today. In the western Catholic Church the sacrament is generally received at an early age. This fact does not allow the once-for-all-time and short-lived event of "being confirmed" to make any lasting impression on an individual.

Perhaps nothing would change very much even if the age for the normal reception of confirmation were to be raised, so this in itself does not resolve the question as to the best age for the reception of confirmation. For the major factor is that no particular attention is lavished on the so-called "sacrament of the Spirit."

Yet it need not be so. Two observations, among others, justify the hope that the sacrament may enjoy a better future. "Charismatic" movements have come into being without and within Catholic Christianity. There is a longing for the experience of the Spirit and its power. Long, charismatically-stirred religious prayer services are held in communities in which worshipers believe they experience the guiding presence of the Spirit—even to the point where they think they have received the gift of tongues. In such periods of prayer many others experience what they call the "baptism in the

Spirit," an exceptional occurrence in which they believe they are possessed by the gifts of the Spirit of God.

Even the most reserved and conservative theology or psychology need not immediately and totally reject such enthusiastic experiences or view them with universal skepticism. Although man, as long as he is still on pilgrimage in time and history, may never regard himself as completely fulfilled, or think that he has received an absolutely sure and definite promise of the Spirit (traditional theology would call this "confirmation in grace"), there is nevertheless no need to dispute the fact that there can be especially striking and liberating experiences of grace, strengthening individuals to make radical transformations in their lives, giving to men and women (and making them feel for a long time) the stamp of Christian life and virtue. Taken all together these can be called (if you will) "baptism of the Spirit." Similarly, whole communities can experience the presence of the Spirit given within a religious service such as prayer.

Why, then, may we not look forward to a new, revitalized understanding of confirmation, the sacrament of the Spirit, on the basis of these experiences bursting forth everywhere in the Church today? There are some who wrongly believe that all the effects of grace and the work of the Spirit are beyond personal experience. Such people dissolve into nothing all religious experience by a rationalistic psychology, considering the life of the Spirit and of grace and of justification in a doctrinaire and *a priori* way. This group is of the opinion that there is no relationship between the sacrament of the Spirit in the dogmatic sense and the experience of "baptism in the Spirit."

Confirmation as the Sacrament of Witness

But there is another and more important consideration: in the Church today, there is a revival of the belief that every Christian has his own special charism for the Church and for the world, a special task of a social and indeed of a "political" kind. But this charism, as far as the Church and profane society alike are concerned, need not necessarily be something "merely profane," a wholly "natural" task. It can also be what we Christians call "grace," a spirit-filled responsibility for others, a concern for the Church and for the world, guided by the Spirit of God. If we do not fall into the trap of regarding religion as something wholly private, of viewing our Christian faith exclusively as a matter between the solitary soul and God, the sacrament of confirmation could take on new importance as the start of our conscious and willed witness to a faith that overcomes the world, and could find a new and more pulsatingly alive future in the Church and in the world.

For confirmation is the sacrament of *mission* and of *witness:* the fulfillment of the task given to us for the Church and for the world. Confirmation need no longer have the trifling existence it possesses in the Church today and which it has been leading for many centuries, despite all the lofty and holy ideas that have been expressed about this sacrament by the official teaching office of the Church and by theologians.

The somewhat trifling existence which confirmation has in the concrete life of the Church is no doubt also conditioned by a theological difficulty which has burdened our understanding of this sacrament from the beginning of Christianity to the present. The difficulty is the following: it is not easy to distinguish between baptism and confirmation. Baptism is not merely a sacrament for the forgiveness of sins and for acceptance of the individual into the Church. It is also the sacrament of rebirth, of the grace-filled inner justification of man, the sacrament of the communication of the Spirit, without which the forgiveness of guilt, rebirth and sanctification cannot even be conceived. And even if one stresses that in confirmation the Spirit is communicated to the recipient for particular tasks and special challenges, for a spiritual strengthening of the person to help him confess his faith

before the world, it must be admitted that the Spirit received
in baptism also confers on the individual the disposition and
strength for undertaking special tasks. We can, to be sure,
point out that according to Biblical texts (Acts 8, 14ff; 19, 6;
Heb. 6, 2), a spirit-conferring imposition of hands was distin-
guished from baptism by early Christians of New Testament
days. But the apparent difficulty is not completely removed
by reference to these texts. For the Spirit-conferring imposition of hands cannot be related to any express mandate of
Jesus. This of course is bound to be of lesser moment today
than it was in the age of the Reformation, because from the
viewpoint of the history of dogma and in the light of the
decisions made by the Council of Trent, we cannot today
deny the institution of the sacrament of confirmation by Jesus
in the Catholic understanding of things. We may, however,
understand the institution of the sacrament in such a way
(once more with the requisite prudence) that it was contained
in the foundation or the origin of the Church begun by Jesus,
so that a categorical foundation by Jesus in historically trans-
mitted words must not necessarily be required with regard to
any of the sacraments, although a foundation of such a kind
with regard to some sacraments ought not be disputed.

If this difficulty of making a distinction between baptism
and confirmation is not so great, we are nevertheless immediately faced with another: the Spirit-conferring imposition of
hands described in the New Testament could indeed be
grasped as a gesture during which an extraordinary charismatic conferral of grace upon individual persons occurred—
something similar to the "baptism in the Spirit," a charismatic "inspiriting" which is simply not bestowed upon all
Christians and therefore cannot pertain to the institutional-
ized means of salvation: the sacraments.

Of course this objection can be countered right away with
the statement that for *all* sacraments (including, therefore,
baptism) a distinction must be made between a fundamental
and sacramental promise of the Spirit making Himself felt in

terms of grace, on the one hand, and the living, powerful efficacy of this Spirit and of this grace announcing themselves in the daily chores of everyday activity. Thus there is no fundamental difficulty in understanding that the Spirit who can be charismatically effective in an imposition of hands as recorded in Acts 8 and 19 can be granted to all. On the other hand, the Spirit operates with visible charismatic power only in special cases, as is evident in the instances cited in the New Testament and as is expected in the enthusiastic movements of contemporary Christianity. We must also make this distinction in the matter of baptism. The difficulty is not so great and overwhelming with regard to the Spirit-conferring imposition of hands in the sacrament of confirmation, as it may at first appear, when we consider that for Paul even very ordinary aptitudes in the service of the community are understood as charismatic gifts of the Spirit. If we understand the effects of the Spirit not as miraculous and "ecstatic matters," but rather as being operative where faith and hope and love bring about a breakthrough of the human being to the freedom of the sons of God in an authentic life, then the imposition of hands in the Acts of the Apostles can be sacramentally understood, while the New Testament sets in bold relief the explicit and marvelous effects of the communicated Spirit.

Even in this perspective, the difficulty of distinguishing between baptism and confirmation and of considering them as two different sacraments still persists. For we must after all understand both sacraments as the communication of the Spirit. Actually, confirmation (as the imposition of hands and anointing, which was considered as Spirit-conferring) was always administered in early Christianity together with baptism or the pouring of water on the head. Thus, our present-day sacrament of confirmation was not originally considered separate from Baptism, as is evident in the Acts of the Apostles. Hence a mere charismatic interpretation of the apostolic imposition of hands might be suggested as the right explanation of many passages.

To resolve this, we will have to go back to an historically impartial understanding of the developments of the sacraments in general, and by so doing consider, as the Council of Trent stresses in its teaching on the sevenfold character of the sacraments that: (1) the individual sacraments are not of the same dignity, (2) not equally necessary for salvation and (3) therefore (as we may add) among themselves need not necessarily be considered separate from one another. Sacraments were founded by Christ. The Church, as the "impenitent" sign of God's unconditional promise to give His Spirit to the world, originates from Jesus, was thus "founded" by Him. Wherever the Church accomplishes Her mission within the individual salvation-situation of any man or woman, whenever She is able to communicate the grace-giving word of salvation that She Herself is, and unconditionally promises to an individual, a sacrament is administered, a sacrament that was founded by Christ, although no specific founding words of Jesus for a definite sacrament can be historically proved or can even be conceived as historically probable.

Confirmation: A Communication of the Spirit

Viewed thus, no difficulty really exists in speaking of the sacraments if one considers that the sevenfold articulation of the one word of grace on the part of the Church is irreversible and final. For the essence of the Church is the communication of the absolute and final word of salvation which She pledges as Her commitment to the world. And She fulfills Her commitment within history through the sevenfold articulation of the sacraments. Thus the sacraments are and remain precisely seven inasmuch as historical decisions of the Church have made them to be such and the decisions are not revocable. It is then altogether understandable that the one fundamental word of grace which the Church savingly promises to man in Baptism is articulated in a twofold way with different explicitness in each case. The Church expressly and unequivocally promises him precisely a communication of the Spirit in confirmation through imposition of hands and anointing, as She had already fundamentally promised it to him in baptism but where it had remained in the background, so to speak, in the first purifying ablutions.

If we wish, then, we can make this twofoldness of the sacramental sign of the conferral of the Spirit in baptism and confirmation easier to understand by asserting that in confirmation this gift of the Spirit is increased and strengthened. It is specified, as it were, for wholly particular tasks of the Christian in the strengthening of his faith for the purpose of bearing witness before the world.

But this explanation, it would appear, is not decisive or final, but only tentative and suggestive. It views the sacramental founding of the Christian life by two opposite sacraments which remain closely related to each other, and are intrinsic parts of the way by which the Church achieves Her purpose of sanctifying the person.

Mention should still be made of some theological data from Scripture and tradition and the teachings of the Church before we make an effort toward still more precise definition of the sacrament of confirmation.

We have already mentioned the Spirit-conferring imposition of hands as recorded in the Acts of the Apostles. In the early Church confirmation was normally administered with baptism. As in the West it was (and remained) the bishop who was the minister of the sacrament, a separation in time ensued between the baptism of children (administered in a later period by simple priests) and confirmation administered at a later age by the bishop. Thus the difference between the two sacraments became distinct.

Medieval councils were acquainted with confirmation-anointing as a sacrament different from baptism. The Council of Trent solemnly defined its sacramentality (1547) without inclusion of a teaching that this sacrament is necessary to salvation. Contemporary Christianity no longer need be troubled with questions about the existence and "sacramentality" of confirmation. On the one hand, Evangelical Christianity has for a long time emphasized the importance of confirmation and stressed the efficaciousness of the grace which the Church proclaims. On the other hand, the Catholic concept of the sacrament, according to which the words of grace as bestowed under the seven signs are valid for them alone, dates only from the Middle Ages and must not hide the difference and the different weight of these seven signs.

According to traditional teaching, confirmation effects a strengthening of faith, completes the grace of baptism and means for the confirmand that he has a permanent "status" in the Church. It is for this reason that the sacrament cannot be repeated, for it confers what is called a "character." Vatican Council II says: "Through the sacrament of confirmation the faithful are more completely united with the Church and provided with a special power of the Holy Spirit. They are in a stricter way obligated to witness to the faith and defend it as true followers of Christ in word and deed." In this, and in other passages, Vatican II emphasizes the special relationship between the sacrament of confirmation and the lay-apostolate.

After these necessary but somewhat academic reflections, we can now seek for that perspective from which the sacrament of confirmation can be better understood today.

Confirmation Today

We should not start with the idea that sacraments are ritual events which effect and give something which otherwise does not exist. If such an idea were our initial point of departure, the question would necessarily arise as to how and where one could sincerely and truthfully experience what has "happened" in the sacraments. Quite naturally, not a few would say that they experienced nothing by way of effect, and the assertion that grace had been granted would be an empty, or at least irrelevant, speculation.

Rather we must proceed, conversely, and ask: Where do we

repeatedly and everywhere in our daily life experience "grace," that reality which elevates and frees our life and which we call the Holy Spirit? The sacraments in these terms can be understood as the promise and fulfillment of precisely this grace, as events that happen in the sphere of existence of the Church. In this sense the Church rules throughout our life and precisely when we are explicitly reached by the sacraments. We must understand the sacraments as the historical and churchly embodiment of grace, which we experience in our daily life, whether or not we expressly call this experience Spirit or grace.

From such a perspective the sacraments are neither superfluous nor unimportant. Rather they appear as the real, churchly presentation of grace. No longer are they seen as a series of particular special events within an otherwise merely earthly, profane and secular world, but rather as its innermost life—a life which gives strength and promises us an eternal future. The efficacy of the sacraments to produce grace is not denied by this view. On the contrary it explicitly embodies itself in the sacraments.

Now it is apropos to ask: Where in our life is that Spirit of the grace of God (whose cultic and socially official promise we perceive in confirmation) concretely operative, though perhaps very discreetly and anonymously? Where in our life is this Spirit, who through this life legitimizes the Spirit-sacrament?

To ask such a question is also to inquire about that "baptism in the Spirit" which, while it sometimes manifests itself in indiscreet and bizarre forms, is being sought by the enthusiastic Spirit movements of our time as the true meaning of Christianity.

We do not need to seek for a baptism in the Spirit, understood as being a datum at a particular point in time, as a unique experience of rebirth, although it should not be denied that such an experience can occur in the life of some Christians. Here we are seeking for more discreet but real attestations of the Spirit of God, on the basis of which we can actually know what is meant by God, His Spirit and His grace.

The Presence of the Spirit

hen a single sustaining hope enables us to face courageously both the enthusiastic highs and the depressing lows of our daily earthly existence; when a responsibility freely accepted continues to be carried out, though it no longer bears any visible promise of success or usefulness; when a human being not only experiences but willingly accepts the last free choice of his death; when the moment of death is recognized as a fulfillment of the promise of life; when we no longer have any proof of the total value of our life's actions, and yet have the strength to view them as positive in God's eyes; when the fragmentary experiences of love, beauty and joy can quite simply be experienced as a continued promise of love, beauty and joy; when the bitter and disappointing and trying events of every day are endured serenely and patiently even to the last day, sustained by a strength whose source is forever elusive; when one dares to pray in silence and darkness and knows that he is heard, without thereafter being able to discuss or dispute his answer; when one deliberately embarks upon total retreat and can experience this as true victory; when falling truly can be called standing; when lack of hope can be seen as a mysterious kind of consolation (without any indulgence in cheap comfort); when one has reached the point of entrusting all his certainty and all his doubts to the silent and encompassing mystery that he now loves above his personal achievements; when . . . (we could continue these examples but it is really up to each one to draw his own personal experiences from the fullness as well as the debris of his daily life)—this is where we truly find God and His liberating grace, where we experience what we Christians call the Holy Spirit, where the difficult but unavoidable experiences of life are welcomed with joy as challenges to our freedom and not as fearful specters against which we try to barricade ourselves in a hell of false freedom to which we are then damned.

Each human being undergoes this experience, although in infinitely different forms and according to his own historical and individual situation. The Christian knows of course that this Spirit of God that is ever present and constantly offered to him for salvation has been promised to mankind in Jesus the Crucified and Risen Lord for the definitive victory of mankind. And the Christian knows that this Spirit has entered into an eternal covenant, one that could never be broken in the long history of mankind. And for this reason the Christian knows that this Spirit, poured out over the world and all flesh and operative everywhere, this Spirit who cannot be ousted from the world by the despairing *No* of the individual human being, is the Spirit of the Father of Jesus, the Spirit of Jesus, a Spirit in whose efficacy and victory we trust, in that we reverently look upon Jesus and His victory in death and in this look no longer dare to disregard the rule of the Spirit in our own life.

There exists a community of those who believe in the victory of God in human history and in the life of the individual, a belief rooted in this reverential look fixed upon Jesus. This community is called the Church. She promises the individual in his life what She Herself is: the palpable and audible explicit Word, which in its Spirit is God as the absolute and happy future of all history and of every individual life.

The Church has already given this Word to us in baptism. But She says it to us (beyond the mere forgiveness of sin) even more distinctly and more urgently in the Word of grace in confirmation, and once again our freedom, as to whether we choose our well-being or our disaster, is awakened and is gently invited to choose life.

Should we not let this Word be spoken to us? Should we not let this Word, in which God promises us His freedom and His own love, the Word that is almost inaudible in the din of everyday life and in the clamor of the markets of pleasure, of politics and of science reporting thousands and thousands of details, be spoken particularly and distinctly and officially in the community of the believers in the Spirit of God? Not exactly for the reason that otherwise we would have nothing to do with this Spirit. Nor for the reason that otherwise we could live more quietly and more comfortably and would not have to undergo the monstrous adventure of searching for our ultimate freedom and the incomprehensibility of God, but rather precisely for the reason that we know that this Spirit inevitably is our fate, for the reason that we once again expressly want to accept and profess this Spirit in our effort to achieve our fullness.

Confirmation, as the sacramental promise and churchly fulfillment of this promise of the Spirit, signifies only a beginning, even if we are confirmed at an age in which our own important life-decisions are taken for a future that is far distant. One cannot really anticipate and pull down the future with all its possibilities into the present moment. Therefore confirmation is also the sacramental sign of a beginning for life, in whose length and breadth the real baptism in the Spirit, all-saving and sheltering within the mystery of God, must occur.

This baptism in the Spirit, which ultimately must be spread over the whole of life, need not be seen in any very spectacular fashion. Wherever responsibility, although no longer of a satisfying nature, is carried out in life; wherever hope struggles against despair and anguish; where love remains; where even guilt is entrusted to God; where death is silently and serenely accepted as promise—there is the baptism in the Spirit of life.

But once we know that such a life, borne by God Himself, is grace, that such life must be bestowed and received as grace, then the explicit profession of our faith becomes something right and necessary. Such a profession of faith, however, occurs in and through penance.

At that holy moment when we hear the liberating promise of the Spirit in Church and experience his call, when we are "confirmed," should we not let this unique word of promise be more and more alive in us for all the future of our life? Should we not preserve its power as something to be constantly renewed and thus become a truly pentecostal people?

Recall that the Spirit promised by the Church through the sacrament of confirmation is the same Spirit who bears the history of nature and the history of mankind as the work of his love and as the dwelling place of his life. Recall that it is the Spirit who forms all true community and who wills to unite all in truth and in love. In this perspective it becomes overwhelmingly clear that the sacrament of the Spirit of confirmation is the sacrament of the witness of faith: a witness given by word of mouth; but especially, and above all, by the testimony of daily life and deeds, that it is the sacrament of Christian mission.

Translated by Salvator Attanasio

3

THE EUCHARIST

The Mystery of Our Christ

W hat happens when we celebrate the Eucharist? The simple answer is: the Lord's Supper which He celebrated at the beginning of His Passion becomes present among us and for us. If we are to understand this central element of our faith we must reflect on what happened at the Lord's Supper, and we must ponder what it means when it is said that this meal becomes present among us and for us.

What did the Lord do when He celebrated the Supper with His apostles? Perhaps the easiest way to place the unfathomable plenitude and impenetrability of this happening before us is to say that in that hour Jesus accepted His death as the giving of Himself to God for the redemption of the world. He gave Himself to God as the one to be put to death and through death submitted to God as the eternal covenant of redemption, and He gave Himself to His disciples in the event and the symbol of a meal.

He sat together with those whom He loved and whom He called His friends and who were for Him the beginning of the community which believed in Him and was to receive salvation in His faith. He sat down with them at table because man is closest to his loved ones when the fellowship of fidelity and love is embodied in the common sharing of bread and drink of the one earth from which all live. He sat together with them for one last time because He knew He had to go, lonesome and alone, to the uttermost darkness and solitude of death. And this death stood hauntingly before Him. His death. The absolute mystery of the incomprehensible. The death of the living One whose being was not, like ours, in a mysterious concurrence with crumbling decrepitude, contradiction, and that nothingness into which guilt tries to escape. Death, the embodiment of guilt, is our destiny, which we simultaneously bring about and endure as the one thing that is peculiarly ours. Jesus accepts this death, He bravely walks toward it, He lets His life of absoluteness, oneness and purity fall into this abyss of infernal meaninglessness with which He has no association. Because the incomprehensibility of Him Whom even in this hour He calls Father ordains it so, because this death is our destiny and because He—eternal, adorable mystery of obedience and love—even in this infinite void and solitude of death wishes to remain one with us and with God.

And together with death He accepts everything else that belongs to this infinity of the dead and of the deadening void: the obtuseness of the hearts of His disciples, their unbelief, the pain, the betrayal, the expulsion from His people, the brutal stupidity of the political policy which wills Him, the failure of His mission and His lifework. He takes hold of the one bottomless cup of His life, looks into the dark abyss and places it to His lips, knowing all and saying Yes to it. He anticipates what we call His Passion, the Passion of the Son of Man: in short, death. This acceptance of the unacceptable, this identification of life with death, this embracing of guilt through holy, obedient love, this descent of the inextinguishable light into the infinite darkness—everything happens within the frame of this quiet and inconspicuous ordinariness of a human life which knowingly walks toward death—is the redemption of the world. It is our salvation, it is the judgment which forgives us, the revelation that we—although cruelly ensnared in our guilt and hopeless desolation—are the accepted and loved ones.

The Passion is begun in the Lord's Supper by Christ's advance acceptance of death in its total and frightening perspectives and by His already proclaiming this acceptance; this acceptance reveals itself in holy gesture and holy word and thus the sacrifice unto real death and the pure devotion to the Father appear in a ritual act of sacrifice.

The Lord stands before His disciples as the One who consecrates Himself to death for them. Only one thing is missing: it has not yet become clear to the disciples that each one of them is wholly and individually included in the acceptance of death by the Lord, that this event of His life-bearing death has penetrated really and truly into the innermost being of each of these disciples, that the fellowship which is theirs and which becomes manifest during the meal reaches into those sinister private recesses of human existence where guilt and death, judgment and eternal responsibility, eternal perdition and eternal redemption reside. Christ gives Himself quite unequivocally and corporeally in the harshest reality of His sacrificed existence, as the Redeemer and the redemption, as death and life.

And thus He says: "Take this body which is given for you, drink this blood poured out for you." And through the power of His creative word which changes the subsoils of reality, He makes Himself exist in the form of bread and wine, the everyday sign of loving unity with his disciples, so that all of this —His sacrificed reality for their salvation—becomes manifest and manifestly operative; it truly belongs to them and enters into the center of their being. "Take, eat; this is my body. Drink . . . for this is my blood of the new covenant which is poured out for all." They take and they are taken. Taken by the redeeming power of obedience and of love of the Lord, taken by His death which gives birth to life out of its dreadful void, encircled by the grace of God which, with the incomprehensible and consuming holiness of God, unites. They are embraced by love which joins them to each other, not destructively but redemptively, enveloped by a love which unites them in an experience where otherwise each would die painfully in himself alone in his ultimate solitude. And by eating the dish of God's mercy, they anticipate the eternal meal when God, no longer in earthly symbols but in the accomplishment of His revealed glory, makes Himself into the eternal meal of the redeemed. And while they eat thus, they look for the day when the Lord will be entirely with them, the day on which He "will come again" (as they say). And the new and eternal covenant which has been bequeathed to them is celebrated as is their free acceptance of it. These are given in the power of this bread which unites them with the Lord Who *is* the covenant and joins them one to another in the beginning of eternal life.

The Lord's Supper becomes His presence among us and for us in the Church's celebration of the Eucharist. The Church fulfills the fundamental order of the Lord: "Do this (what He Himself had done on the night He was betrayed) in remembrance of Me." The Church does what the Lord had done, with the words which He Himself spoke when He gave His body and His blood in the form of bread and wine to His disciples as a pledge of eternal life. The Church celebrates the Anamnesis, the "remembrance" of the meal that instituted the new covenant. The Church recalls what once happened but does not bring about a repetition of the actual event which happened once and for all on Calvary. Rather, what happened then enters into our place and our time, and acquires presence and redemptive power within our own being.

This is possible (if we may so try to understand the miracle of God) because the Lord's Supper is not an event of the past. The free decision of absolute obedience and unconditional, unreserved love constitutes one of those moments of history in which a temporality becomes the definitive, the enduring and the eternal, not just a moment in which something evaporates into the void of the past. The elements of freedom and spirit always signify the birth of the eternal; in this context, what is temporal passes into time but also attains eternal validity by virtue of the pure essence of the decision itself by a spiritual person. This applies in an utterly unique way to the event of the Last Supper. What happened there as event once and for all is. It *is*. It is taken up in the eternity of God, it has passed over into the state of perfection in which it becomes permanence in the midst of time. For the Lord in this meal has wrought something that endures forever since His voluntary deeds come from the infinite primal grounds of the eternal *Word of God* itself and are a spiritual-human reality, like the creative words of Genesis. He has wrought the "new" and thus the final covenant, as He Himself says.

Thus He *is* the One whom He became in that time in His passion, ever and eternal: the crucified One and the resurrected One, the eternal grounds for trusting oneself to the mystery of God, the lover who experienced the deepest helplessness of being human and endured all futility of utter devotion until it became victory itself. He *is* the one He became, and when we in holy Anamnesis proclaim His death until He comes again, we are not relating an incident from the scattered past, but proclaiming the once and for all presence with eternal validity.

What is past in this death that was accepted at the Supper is but what perforce had to pass away so that eternal presence could be. In the resurrected and glorified Lord we find the validity of His history become present and remaining so. And such a present is His redeeming death—death overcome in the dead and resurrected Lord present among us, in our time and in our life. Indeed this event of His redemptive death accepted at the Supper embraces our life always and everywhere. We are always the many for whom One died. We are always those who have been redeemed, absolved by God, our life is always grounded upon this one event. But it calls for our decision, it asks for our freedom, it needs to be accepted by us in faith. And therefore this enduring event, accomplished once and for all, is forever valid, and remains the enduring law of our life for our salvation or our perdition. It aspires to become part of our time and our place, to penetrate

33

the surface of our being in order to call forth our faith, to make it possible and to sustain it.

That is why we celebrate the Lord's Supper in a ritual and concrete way, that is why He is present in the celebration of the Holy Communion which the Church performs as He performed it, in obedience to His will that instituted the Eucharist in the first place: to give Himself, His body and His blood as food to those who believe in Him, who love Him and who enter into the mystery of His death. When the Church does what He did and enjoined us to do, then He is there among us: there in His corporeal person there is the High Priest of His community before the God of all worlds and of history, there as our own sacrifice because He sacrificed Himself for us and we, before the majesty of the holy God, are entitled to appeal to the obedience and the love of our Lord, as our sacrifice Who has put Himself in our hands, so that our ritualistic celebration, as a liturgical and sacrificial gesture, makes manifest anew what happened once and for all in the sacrifice of His life to the eternal God. He is present as the gift which enters into us as the pledge of eternal life. He is present as the unity of love among us. He is present with His death and the life which He won from death. He is present as the beginning of the transfiguration of the world and as the pledge of the irrestible irruption of the glory of God in the darkness of sin. He is there as the power of life and as the power which sweeps us up into His death in order to bless our death with His life. He is there as the friend and fellow-traveler, as the brotherly sharer of our destiny. And in all this in which He is present among us and for us, He establishes Himself in us, He takes us into Himself while we receive Him. The eternal validity of His life and death and the promise of our future become sacramentally one in our presence. One thing only is demanded of us: the "amen" of our living faith for the deed the Lord has accomplished for us.

When we say Yes, when we co-celebrate, when we let ourselves be seized in faith and love by what is happening among us and to us, we ourselves are contained in the Yes of the Son to the unfathomable ordinance of the Father, we are the ones who praise and we are the ones who offer thanks and sacrifice, we are those who are sacrificing and are sacrificed, but sacrificing and sacrificed in that sacrifice which alone does not evaporate into empty meaninglessness. Then we are worshipers in spirit and in truth, then we are the unified being beyond all dissension and inner strife. We are the transformed for which the law that killeth has been transformed into the freedom of the spirit, death into life, time into validity. When we accept Him all is absorbed into the infinity of God and the love of Christ, everything becomes reconciled, everything opens up, everything finds its solution. Like every other sacrament this too becomes operative in us, the free, only it does so in proportion to our faith and in such a way that precisely this faith is received from the grace of God. His affirmation enters our lives tangibly in this "sacrament of faith," in this *mysterium fidei*, so that faith and sacrament mutually sustain each other because both are sustained by the grace of God in Christ which this sacrament has effected: the presence of the Lord and His expiatory death.

Whatever this sacrament of sacrifice is, it *is* as the sacrifice and the received sacrificial food, as the Christ who entrusted Himself to the Father and entrusted Himself as food to us. The Lord gave Himself to us precisely as food to be enjoyed. According to His own words, what He offers is His body and blood so that we may receive Him. That is why the heavenly food for eternal life, like earthly food, can be preserved for partaking by the hungry and thus by its very being entices and attracts us to receive it. Thus the embodied meal of love can be offered to others than those who could be physically present at its first preparation. That is why the Church, at no time of its history, has ever forbidden the preservation of the consecrated bread in the midst of Her faithful, so that it could serve, outside the great feast of sacrifice of the community, as the bread of life for the individual.

The Church has always been of the conviction that in this way one could always participate in the feast of sacrifice of the community, in the celebration of the Eucharist. And because the Church knows that in this preserved sacrament, according to the words of Christ, the Lord is truly and substantially present in flesh and blood, in body and soul, in divinity and humanity, She has increasingly learned to venerate this sacrament of Her Lord, the word of the Father become flesh, and to worship it to embrace it with that devotion and love due the Savior and Lord of the Church. The Eucharistic piety outside the celebration of the Mass has certainly grown in the course of history, and at times it has assumed forms and configurations which brought with them the danger that the crucial and most primal realities would be concealed by pious exuberances of love. The whole of the history of such Eucharistic piety, however, is but a fraction of the proper practices which have been introduced, and which will doubtless lead to new and deathless insights in the enduring action of the Church.

The silent adoration of the Lord by the single believer who kneels in front of the holy shrine on our altars, the presentation of the sacrament in the monstrance by which the mystery is "exposed" to our eyes, rightly understood, need not necessarily lead away from the significance of the sacrament. On the contrary, in this way too the food proclaims the eternal life of our dying Lord; and venerated precisely in this way, it calls us to partake of it. When the mystery of Christ always and everywhere encompasses our being (whether or not we heed it), why should this secret of our being not be allowed to become visible so that our eye may fall on the food of the Church, in which one eats life or judgment?

We are always (to the extent that only the spirit of Christ lives in us and moves us) in spiritual communication with Christ (or we could be), whether we kneel in church or walk the dusty streets of everyday life. But this spiritual communication is also our *task*. The enduring sacrament reminds us to take up this task. In it the word of God, which calls us to abide in Christ and in His love (and offers the strength for it) becomes ever clearer and unmistakable. "Extra-sacramental" Eucharistic piety always remains united with its source, with the celebration of the sacrificial banquet. It remains rich in content and it is sound when it remembers this relation to the sacrifice of the Mass.

From this point of view one is able to understand what Catholic Christendom does on the feast of Corpus Christi or at a Eucharistic Congress. Such a day is not a day of demonstration against the belief of other Christians. If one viewed it thus (on one side or the other), one would be misinterpreting the meaning of this sacrament which is the bond of unity and love and should become this more and more. This celebration therefore cannot have such a meaning if only for the reason that the custom of the feast of Corpus Christi goes back to a time when there was no schism in western Christianity. The feast has its roots in the ancient field processions. In them man walks along the earthly dimensions of his life, carrying the "Holy" (the relics of the Church included the "Holy of Holies") into his whole world.

Because everything in its abundance grows out of *one* root and reaches out for one end, in the procession man entwines the spaces and the accomplishments of his being: the vast openness of the world becomes a church, the sun is the altarlight, the fresh wind sings with the songs of man, the altars stand on the corners of everyday life, the sober congregation of people standing before God becomes the gay and colorful procession of the marchers and the carefree birds of heaven execute their flight right through the prayer which rises from the afflicted earth, already almost transmuted into pure songs of praise. And when the Christians of the Church walk this way through the spaces of their everyday existence, they want to carry along, they want to show, what in this movement of their existence, becomes tangible and visible, sustains them through the changeable to the enduring, what is already the sign and the promise, the sacramental presence of that toward which there are heading, the eternal salvation, infinite rest, life that no longer declines. The goal incorporates all movement into itself and changes it. And that is why they carry with them the sacrament of their altars. It is as if they want a closer confrontation with the irritating and wicked profaneness of their big-city daily life, in the very quarries of these cities with the silent Blessed Sacrament which otherwise is shyly hidden in the shrines of the churches, and in which they themselves stand helpless and lost somewhere in the endless sea of houses.

Naturally the *decisive* confrontation of the profane, guilty world in need of redemption with the eternal and gentle power of the grace of God can take place only in the hearts of men. But Christendom wants to express, wants to make apparent, that this grace desires to save, to sanctify and to redeem the life and not merely the vague and private longings of man. And that is why Christendom carries the sacrament of eternal life into the midst of the ordinariness of the unhallowed world. This procession says: "We have the Crucified and Resurrected Jesus with us on this pilgrimage through the world. He goes with us right through our life on all its paths. He meets us in the destinies which befall us at the crossroads of our paths. Unknown He looks at us through the brother whom we indifferently pass by. We carry through our streets the sign of the presence of Him who is the way and the goal, of Whom we profess that all paths become straight and purposeful if only He goes with us."

We are Christians. But that means that we must ever anew and ever more truly become what indeed we are. The eternal new beginning of such new becoming is the confession that we are still at the start of our journey and that a long way still lies in front of us. Thus it is also with respect to our understanding of the holy sacrificial meal which Christ left to His Church, and thereby to us, as the holy Anamnesis of His suffering. We may calmly acknowledge that spirit and heart in us and still have scant understanding of this mystery in which the whole mysterium of Christianity is gathered. It is not surprising that the narrowness of our being gives way only with great difficulty to this divine reality. But it would be horrible indeed if we were to make this narrowness of our being a standard of our thinking and if we were to become indifferent to, or irritated by, or even incredulous of the infinite challenge of truth and fence ourselves up in the dull dailyness of our lives.

It would be pitiful if we were to reconcile ourselves forever to the inadequate and perhaps half-magical misconceptions of this sacrament which we drag along with us from early religious instruction and from the practices of our childhood. We should learn to understand what we do when we participate in the celebration of the Mass, when we accept the sacrament. This act should be more than the act performed out of a vague need to insure ourselves against God and to fulfill some legalistically interpreted demands of religion only by a dimly understood religious practice. Here is the mystery of the absolute nearness of God, the mystery of His Christ, the sacrament of His death, the sacrifice of His Church, the power of life, the bond of unity and love, the forgiveness of daily sinfulness, the promise of eternal life, the precelebration of eternity, the new and eternal covenant between God and His creation, the event of the tender meeting of the heart with the God of hearts, the acceptance of death and of life. All this reality, to be sure, always encompasses our life and, perhaps, penetrates to the very middle of its most everyday misery as our eternity in our being, in our heart: in an hour of unconditional fidelity, in the darkness of death, in the blissfulness of love (who is able to say when God victoriously surmounts the walls of our disbelief?). But precisely this mystery of our being appears in this sacrament as that which it is, whereas we overlook or misinterpret it in other forms.

And that is why the Christian cannot say that the communion of life with God does not need the communion with God under the sacramental sign, about which exactly the same must be said as pertains to the mystery of our life. The growing consecration of both in one is the task of our life. It will take us a long time before we really and genuinely will have understood what is so easily said concerning this sacrament. We should entreat God for the grace to understand what we celebrate in faith, illuminated in spirit and heart to accept what we receive with the mouth. And God who offered us the gift will also give us the understanding of the gift without which the gift itself will not bear fruit.

If we find it difficult to find the right approach to the inner understanding of this sacrament, we have to search our own souls. Let us pose to ourselves the mystery of our own life from which we flee in the hustle and bustle of our everyday life and through the narcotics of our pleasures! Let the infinite longing take power in us! Hearken to the indwelling death in us! Let us be horrified over the cruel loneliness of the human being locked up in us! Let us seriously ask if the insensibility to God which we have tried to assess as an accusation against Him, or as half-admitted proof against His existence, is not really that with which we have allied ourselves deep down in our hearts, so that we do not have to become men of infinite love, men of eternity who blissfully let God make exorbitant demands on them. If in this or similar ways (there are innumerable more) we undeviatingly resist our own true selves, we will suddenly receive an understanding of this sacrament. For what we hear from Him in faith will suddenly sound as the answer to the question which came up in us, which is our selves. Do we suffer from the distance from God? Here is the voice of Him who spoke in the utter darkness of death: Father, into Thy hands I commit my spirit. Here He is with His death! Do we suffer from the pain of being unable to love? Here is the One who in the night when He was betrayed (He was betrayed by us all) loved His disciples up to the end. Would we like to be loyal to the earth and no longer see the works of this earth perish? Here is the

transfigured world in the transfigured flesh of the Resurrected, here is the beginning of the glorious validity of this earth! Take and eat the pledge of the salvation and glorification of all flesh! Are we tormented by the ambiguity, the fragility and hollowness of our own being, its guilt, its failure, its horrendous wretchedness? Here is the One who has suffered for us, as He was without guilt, through all the abysses of our guilt, since He became a curse for us, who, knowing us to our abysses, accepted us, loved us, healed us! Are we tormented by the fear of meaningless decay and destruction? Here is the One who has anticipated all meaningless decay and destruction, Who has redeemed them and Who gives us power in pure powerlessness to accept them. Here is everything: the meaning, the pain and the bliss of our existence. Hidden, however, and open only to faith. But truly and really. O holy banquet, thus will we pray with the Church, in which Christ is received, in which His suffering in commemorating celebration is made present, and in which is given the pledge of our approaching glory.
Amen.

Translated by Salvator Attanasio

4

PENANCE

Allow Yourself to Be Forgiven

If we wish to make pointed, brief and meaningful observations on the sacrament of penance, we must deal immediately with a profoundly obscure, even incomprehensible sphere of man's life and of his history: with his guilt.

There exists for man one mystery of complete and enduring incomprehensibility: God. It is precisely within this illuminating and sheltering mystery of God's incomprehensibility that man, through faith and hope and love, entrusts himself to become free and happy. On another level, the experience of mankind and even more strongly Christian faith point to still another mystery: the ever deepening guilt of man who has not achieved the objective of his personal freedom within the incomprehensibility of God. The existence of this obscure mystery of guilt attains its final meaning for man only when he turns to God in a true conversion. Origen, that most influential biblical scholar and theologian of the early Greek church, showed how closing oneself off to grace and amnesia of the Word pertain to the peculiarity of true guilt itself, without thereby cancelling it. According to Christian teaching, difficult as it may be to conceive, there can really be a free *No* to God which basically amounts to destroying the relationship of man to himself, to his fellow man and to the things of this world. It is, however, really a *No* to God which ultimately—even though it is not necessarily thought out and thematized—strives in isolation toward its own finality and irrevocability. This in fact is what it achieves if man's effort to be free is cut off by death. In that case the result of the final and free *No* to God is what we call judgment and definitive perdition.

What is "Guilt before God"?

That a result of this kind comes about through a merely finite freedom, one which even in the very commission of the guilty deed was motivated by a search for the Good in general and which was also subject to the most manifold variety of circumstances and conditions of man in all the dimensions of his life—that is really an incomprehensible mystery. But it is a mystery, assuredly, whose fundamental denial would abolish the very dignity of man—the dignity of responsibility and of true love and of freedom. For these things do not signify merely the faculty to choose between particular finite goods of the world, but rather freedom vis-a-vis the ultimate position of man as a complete person, and vis-a-vis the absolute future of man, the ground of his freedom and, finally, vis-a-vis the greatest mystery of all: God.

Wherever this kind of guilt actually exists, and this itself is an area of mystery about which we can make no judgment, it is not a question of a particular decision to go contrary to the regulations of this or that individual; nor is it a question of one or another particular kind of foolishness or error which, given the finiteness and conditionality of man, are never lacking in his life. No matter who we are, we will always find ourselves subject to mistakes, and in the process of learning how to use freedom as our lives are scattered through space and time. Rather, it is a question of an ultimate, irrevocable protest, stemming from the rejection of life itself, of an act against oneself as a whole person and against God.

Where this kind of protest is not found, even in an unthematic and unreflected form in the ultimate depths of our existence and of our original freedom, there can be no talk of the kind of guilt actually meant here. One cannot understand its real, unique and incomparable essence if one fixes one's attention simply on the occurrences of everyday life, in which an individual "consciously" and "freely" violates particular individual regulations which stand under the keeping of an external punitive authority. Of course, we cannot altogether avoid the consideration of particular acts, but these acts do not amount to the real essence of guilt before God. Guilt before God is not just a collection of minor infractions and transgressions of the law. Just as we cannot say that God (when one really grasps what is meant by this word) is an individual particular reality (although of the mightiest kind) among and alongside other individual realities which constitute our world, in the same way we cannot define guilt before God as a combination of infractions of the law that we might possibly commit against human norms and authorities, even though we fundamentally recognize the latter as quite legitimate.

The Totality of Factors in "Guilt before God"

Once again: that real guilt before God as we have defined it can actually exist, that is an incomprehensible mystery. And especially for the reason that we, despite all the wretchedness and horror in the world and in history, can never point a finger at a wholly particular event and say with clear and final certitude: here is guilt before God. As Christians, of course, we can and we must say that the cross and the death of Jesus have their cause in real *guilt*. Nevertheless, we do not know with absolute certainty that any particular individual is in a state of final depravity and perdition, was not saved by the mercy of the cross of Jesus. We cannot in the last resort distinctly localize guilt, the "sin of the world," which plunged Jesus into death; we cannot state that it exists in wholly particular and unique persons and deeds and distinguish exactly between the ultimately naive characters on the stage of history we view and the real authors of this profound guilt full of eternal damnation.

The modern world, through its sciences of psychology, depth-psychology, the social sciences and other studies, has discovered thousands and thousands of things that condition man, things which in individual cases justifiably warrant posing the question as to whether here and now real ultimate guilt before God exists. It is self-evident that wrong things are done and done again, but whether or not guilt before God exists, we can never truly say because of the host of forces that come to bear on the particular person before us. We see the horror and the destructive deeds of man, but should this monstrousness of human "crime" be reckoned only among those monstrosities of the world and history which, by the will of God, exist in the form of plagues, famines, in the degenerative processes of the biological life of man, etc., we will never know. And we cannot, in the last resort, exculpate God from such horrors of nature in human history by appealing to "original sin" because by so doing the problem of God's permission of guilt would but be shifted to another area of debate —it would still not be comprehensible why the consequences of original sin should also strike those who are personally innocent, except that God does indeed strike persons whom He loves and to whom He also communicates a radical will to salvation in Christ.

We human beings are always tempted to try to assess real guilt before God, with all its radical consequences, especially where terrible deeds of others personally strike *us* and where they diminish or destroy the "unbroken" and peaceful world that we would like to have. But when we ourselves do something wrong, something under pressure from the most varied external circumstances, something definitely wrong but not attended by the gruesome consequences of the great "crimes of world history;" something "innocently" wrong, but which in its ultimate cause and by quiet evaluation of our innermost dispositions is hardly different from the cause of those world-shattering crimes and something which might give us pause to wonder about the extent of the "Hitler in us," then we are only too easily inclined to utilize all the reasons placed at our disposal by the various sciences to absolve ourselves from real, radical guilt before God. By so doing we are certainly not always wrong. There are thousands of reasons coming from our natural endowments, our social milieu, the abortive qualities of our upbringing, our genes, coercive social pressures, public opinion, the alleged limitedness of our motivation, etc., which in many cases rightly absolve us. But even here, as well as in the case in which we assume and acknowledge our free guilt and recognize that we are answerable to God for our behavior, it it still not always absolutely certain that we have or have not committed a sin. For (disregarding all else) the totality of motivations of a deed and whatever in it we reflectively and clearly grasp and have thoughtfully made our own, is not identical with the truth. Therefore, no one can say with absolute certainty and cocksureness, whatever appearances may suggest in a particular case, that one is really guilty or not guilty. According to the Gospel we cannot in a concrete and individual case, judge ourselves or others with absolute certainty in the matter of guilt before God. We have no doubt the right and the obligation to draw practical conclusions from a human judgment of a deed (of one's own and, under broader presuppositions, of one committed by others) as such a judgment not only is possible for us, along with all its problematic aspects, but also unavoidable. A murderer for example is punished by society. We consider ourselves obliged to make restitution even though such an obligation arises only in cases of real guilt, and all we are able to do with certainty is to make a sacramental charge of guilt and so forth. But the fact remains: an absolute judgment on a real guilt before God in a determined individual case is not possible to man. We can cite no concrete case of guilt in which it is clearly and without doubt certain that an act involves guilt before God and is worthy of damnation. It follows that in daily Christian life we cannot define in any distinct and concrete way the line between trust and hope on the one hand, and fear on the other, in regard to our salvation. We cannot by ourselves distinguish between sheep and goats. We cannot anticipate the world-judgment of God. For this reason the history of the Church and of her saints is never a nursery tale of unalloyed good untouched by the fear of possible harm or evil done to others.

This situation of man, defined by the impossibility of making a distinct judgment between good and evil (which is something different from the distinction between earthly and human competence and incompetence) is no license for him to indulge in the naive optimism that the world is assuredly not so bad; that although there is, admittedly, much monstrousness in the deeds of men, the latter is, in the last analysis and despite appearances, the monstrousness of a "nature" anteceding freedom for which not man but God is answerable and from which, finally, God is bound to draw good.

Although this monstrousness of nature (heredity, the harsh laws of psychology, social coercions, etc.) is mixed up with the monstrousness of freedom in all human history, and in a way that is not analyzable by us, so that we always apparently have sufficient grounds to dissolve the monstrousness of freedom in the monstrousness of nature and thus exonerate ourselves, the evil of freedom in the world still exists according to Christian conviction. And precisely because evil cannot be totally isolated nor limited to wholly particular individual points in the history of the individual or mankind the human situation is difficult to deal with. This real evil of guilt before God can also hide itself behind an apparent good, behind those innocuities about which people say that He who understands everything, can also forgive everything. A seemingly harmless burgeoning of personal development (possibly at a relatively young age) can (which does not mean must) be the seemingly harmless though still undefined surface and facade of a life-decision toward really evil guilt.

If real guilt (which is not at all clear in personal self-analysis) could be pinned down to one particular point in a person's life; if this apparently deliberate guilt at one particular point in the individual's life were but the inexorable consequence of an earlier decision (made freely but lacking in total reflection and perspective); and if, notwithstanding, according to Christian fundamental conviction, this real evil of guilt before God does exist, then the Christian could regard his whole life with a holy and a cautious skepticism. Then for him the distinction between the mere possibility and the actual reality of free evil in his own life (which after all is not concretely and clearly practicable to make) would not be so important. For with his whole being, which he grants is ultimately not able to be judged by him, he could flee to God, to Divine mercy and forgiveness. The test of life, the examination of conscience, the distinction between good and evil actions will always relate to an authentic human and therefore also to a Christian life, because we do what we consider proper, and only that which has been done and remains forever dark is entrusted silently and hopefully to God.

The Hopelessness of Guilt

Before we can proceed from this uncancellable dark situation of our existence to the hoped-for word of the forgiveness of God and reflect upon this word as it is uttered by the Church, there is still another consideration to ponder: the impossibility by man alone of cancelling human guilt, especially where such guilt really exists or can exist in the sense we have defined. This impossibility of cancelling real guilt must not be understood in the fashion of a transgression which an individual in civil society commits against another and for which he is answerable, even though he may regret this transgression and ardently wish that it had never come about.

Similarly it is irrelevant whether the transgression inflicted a material damage or constituted an offense against personal dignity.

In both cases an offense has been done and cannot simply be wished away. This impossibility of cancelling guilt must be understood precisely in the context that a conversion to God, a free distancing of oneself vis-a-vis the earlier decision inasmuch as it is the deed alone of man as such, still does not bring about a cancellation of the guilt. Of course, when and where there is a true conversion to God, God's merciful turning toward the penitent and His willingness to forgive are already latent with the factors involved in cancellation of guilt and its forgiveness, except that the fact of remorse and sorrow are required on the part of the sinner. The hopelessness of guilt flowing from the recognition of guilt itself constitutes its own dark mystery, one that is interpretable only with great difficulty.

It is precisely the accepted experience of this hopelessness and the desire to transcend it which pertain to the mystery of guilt and that are already a kind of beginning of conversion. The hopeless impossibility of cancelling guilt is initially grounded (insofar as one can attempt a closer explanation) in the dialogic peculiarity of the existence of man in relation to God. If this relationship is the result of a free act, involving an openness to God's giving and a wish to respond, then such a positive relationship between God and man is not reestablished only through the fact that the guilty man tries to take back his *No* to God. The salvation-bearing love between God and man is so constituted, through the free gift of God, that man must again return to the roots of his own love for God, despite the fact that it is given in freedom, as a very gift of the free love of God to him. The personal self-opening and self-communication of God in His love for man is in itself, and as an act enabling us to love Him, the freedom of God and ever remains so, whether or not one wishes to understand such a love bestowed upon the sinner on the path to conversion as an unattestable continuance of an original love or as a *new* turning of God towards the sinner.

This freedom of the love of God, however, still does not constitute by itself the ground for the impossibility of man's own cancelling of his guilt. Further factors, implicitly contained in this freedom of divine love, must be made clearer so that, in some fashion, we may grasp this hopelessness of guilt in its own terms.

We have already said that the essence of human freedom could not be understood if we were to grasp it as a constantly-open faculty of choice, which could be revised at will and thus floats in a void. Freedom is, essentially, despite its temporal historicity, the will to that which is definitive and final. Only thus can we understand why the brief life-span of man can create a meaningful finality of salvation or perdition. For we cannot conceive of God as the One who, from the outset, arbitrarily rejects or accepts freedom, or, in Christian terms, follows man around as the judge of ever-continuing transgressions. Hence a concrete experience of freedom becomes comprehensible when a man, even though he still stands in the open time of history, does not look upon his past actions as a once and for all time completed corruption, and yet does not consider them cancelled simply because he now plans to do that which is contrary to his past actions.

The Word of Forgiveness

If a man understands his earlier stages of freedom as lasting and binding, and also regards his forgetfulness or "change of heart" as powerless in the eyes of God Who was always involved in his life, then he does not exaggerate the importance of his past, and experiences the reality and mystery of his freedom. One can make the mystery of the "externalness" of a free act more comprehensible by distinguishing between a transitory act and its enduring consequences. But even this obscures the mystery of the free act, the "eternalness" of which pertains to God alone: it is God's love that really cancels the guilt itself, a guilt whose incomprehensibility pertains to the incomprehensibility of God.

Before we directly ponder the forgiving word of God, reference should be made to the traditional Christian teaching between grievous or mortal sin and venial sin. This distinction is quite legitimate since the freedom of man, which is constantly at work throughout his entire life, does not always play an active role in the final act of man (in which an absolute *Yes* or *No* to God could exist); and because, furthermore, in all the multiplicity of man's actions, which vary in degree of importance, there is not always at man's disposal one single act of sufficient magnitude through which an absolute *Yes* or *No* to God can be communicated.

As correct as this distinction is in itself, however, it must not be understood too accommodatingly. From what we said earlier, no simple answer is possible in relation to the question as to whether a mortal or mere venial sin exists in a particular case. An ultimate unbelief and a loveless hardening of the heart toward God, which can really endanger salvation, can also hide behind a bourgeois respectability in which only seemingly harmless transgressions are recognized. The distinction between both kinds of sins—which is one of essence and not of degree—of which only one "excludes a person from the kingdom of heaven" (as Paul says) can in practice be very important in relation to the question as to whether a particular guilt should or should not be subjected to the churchly court of penance in the "confession." The difficulty of decision, however, makes it meaningful to turn to the sacramental rite of forgiveness in the Church, even though one may have only "venial" sins to confess.

When we have really understood what guilt is, as both a possibility or as a terrible reality, and what it signifies in our life; when we have experienced how hopeless real guilt before God (deriving from man alone) really is, then we desire to hear God's word of forgiveness. We will never experience it as self-evident, but rather as a miracle of His mercy and His love. We would not understand God at all, if we were to think, as Heine cynically expressed it, that it is God's "metier" or job to forgive. Forgiveness is the greatest and most incomprehensible miracle of the love of God because in it God communicates Himself to a human being who in the seeming banality of everyday life has had the effrontery to say *No* to God.

Where is this word of God's forgiveness to be heard, a word which is not only the consequence but also the precondition for the conversion in which the guilty, believing, penitent human being trustingly turns to God and surrenders himself to Him? This gentle word of forgiveness can be heard in the depths of the conscience because it already dwells in it as supportive ground in that trusting and loving turning back of man to God—a turning back in which man, judging himself, honors the merciful love of God.

In the vast length and breadth of mankind's history this gentle word of forgiveness must suffice by itself alone in countless cases. But there is more: for God's love has made itself especially evident in the history of man's conscience, hidden and unarticulated in most cases. The mercy of God has offered to all salvation and forgiveness within space and time, for the word of God's forgiveness has become concrete in space and time and has found its total expression and its rich historical irrevocability in Jesus Christ, the crucified and risen Lord. He, the Loving One of God became one with all sinners and in His final act of faith, hope and love experienced in the darkness of His own death the darkness of our guilt and accepted for us God's word of forgiveness.

This word of God's forgiveness in Jesus Christ—one in which the unconditionality of this word has also become historically evident and irrevocable—remains present in the community of those believing in this forgiveness, in the Church. The Church is the fundamental sacrament of this word of God's forgiveness.

This one word of forgiveness, which is the Church, and which remains in Her living presence of power and efficacy, is heard in manifold ways consonant with the essence of man. As a fundamental message it is present to all in the proclamation of the Church: *I believe . . . in the forgiveness of sins,* as we read in the profession of faith of the Apostles' Creed. This word of forgiveness of the Church is promised in a fundamental way to the individual by the Church in the sacrament of baptism and remains basic and decisive for the whole history of an individual. This word of forgiveness remains alive and efficacious in the prayer of the Church, in which, ever anew and confidently, She solicits the mercy of God for every individual and thus everywhere and always accompanies the conversion of man, always becoming more complete and more profound up to the final victory in the moment of death. This word of forgiveness (always building upon the word pronounced in baptism) is promised to the individual once again by the Church and in a special way, where and when the Christian, who also remains a sinner after baptism and can fall into a state of new grievous guilt, contritely confesses his great guilt or the wretchedness of his life to the Church in Her representative or possibly acknowledges it in a common confession of a community before God and His Christ. When this word of forgiveness of God is spoken to an individual baptized person based on his confession of guilt, we call this event of the forgiveness-creating word of God the administration of the sacrament of penance.

Insofar as this efficacious word of forgiveness is promised to the already baptized member of the Church on the basis of his confession, it has a definite specificity: the baptized Christian, as a link in the Church, has in his "major" or "minor" guilt placed himself in contradiction to the essence of the holy community to which he belongs, the Church, whose existence and life ought to be signs that the mercy of God as love for God and man together is victorious throughout the world. Through Her word of forgiveness the Church thus "loosens" the wrong that the guilt of man does to the Church. Indeed, one may say the Church forgives guilt through God's word of forgiveness entrusted to Her, in that She forgives man the wrong done to Her, even as She communicates the Holy Spirit of the Church in the baptism of man, in that the Church incorporates Him within Herself as the Body of Christ. The reason is that this word of forgiveness of the Church is pronounced within the concrete guilt-situation of the individual as the word of Christ and with the definitive engagement of the Church, consonant to Her essence; it is not only a verbal utterance of the forgiveness of God, but rather its actuality; this word is really a sacrament.

This is what is reported in Mt. 16, 19 and 18, 18 and in Jn. 20, 20–23: the Church in the remission of sins loosens "on earth" (i.e. in Her domain), so that man is also loosened "in heaven" (in the remission of his guilt before God). In such an event, great mercy is declared and effected through the sacramental sign of the human word of forgiveness (a forgiveness that can be effected and is effected outside this sign too through the mercy of God where men obediently subject themselves to the holy dictates of their conscience). The sacramental character and the binding quality of this churchly word of forgiveness in the matter of an existing grievous guilt is as irrevocable for God and for man as the forgiveness of a baptized person, but guilt is as little cancelled as the sacramental character, efficaciousness and necessity of baptism—according to the teachings of all Christian churches—is cancelled by the fact that a man can already be justified in faith, hope and love and be filled with the Spirit of God, where through no fault of his own he does not know of the necessity of baptism and rise through baptism as a justified person. In both sacraments, pursuant to God's will, there should be manifest in His Word Become Flesh that which His mercy forgivingly and holily effects in the depths of human existence.

The Teaching of the Church

The sacramental character of this word of forgiveness of the Church vis-a-vis the individual had been solemnly defined at the Council of Trent (1547 and 1551). It was also established there that in the case of objective and subjective guilt, of which the individual is sure judging by reasonable human standards, a duty exists to submit this guilt to the sacramental word of forgiveness of the Church. Where such a grievous guilt, even a subjective one, is considered not present with sufficient sureness, there exists no duty to make a sacramental individual confession, nor even an "annual confession." On the basis of what has been said and on the basis of the practice and recommendation of the Church, it equally holds true that a sacramental forgiveness of sins is nevertheless significant and helpful, even if a strict obligation to its sacramental forgiveness does not exist. Whether in such cases an individual confession or participation in a "penitential devotion" of the community is more recommendable and more salutary depends on the subjective disposition of the individual and on the ceremonies of the particular community.

Whether a grievous guilt is forgiven in an individual confession, whether a man receives the word of forgiveness of the Church for his "venial sins," whether through faith and hope and love in the everyday actions of his life and his supplication in the Our Father—*forgive us our trespasses*—an individual's cry for help is heard, two things at any rate must be recognized, must be realized according to the best of one's abilities. First and foremost a true conversion to God is only possible in the measure in which a man overcomes the guilt that he has committed against his neighbor. Every kind of guilt, in some sense and some extent, actually has the aspect of a violation of the duty to love one's neighbor. Even our wholly hidden evil thoughts effect an inner disposition, which inexorably impels us toward violations in actual fact against the injunction to love one's neighbor. To that extent every kind of guilt has a "social" aspect. If the latter is to be taken into account in the turning away from guilt, then this turning away at least in very many cases cannot content itself with mere regret over our earlier deeds.

The concrete practical relationship to our neighbor must be cleansed. At the same time it must not be forgotten that a great amount of injustice and lovelessness exists in the world, for which we are responsible, but which do not at all become discernible in the average everyday consciousness of man and of society: the exploitation of social power for one's own advantage, the culpable economic advantages which play into the hands of the unjust structures of our society and are all too matter-of-factly and selfishly accepted. Such and similar sins against love of neighbor and justice must be pondered and overcome, even though they do not at all occur in the customary confessional manuals. If the "peace with the Church," which is an inner factor of forgiveness in the sacrament of penance, is not to become just a fruitless ideology, then the Christian must understand that such peace with the Church is only truth and reality when it rests upon a very sober and realistic effort to bring about more justice and love in everyday life. Therefore a penitential devotion should not succumb to the danger of becoming once again a liturgically pre-planned ritual. Rather, it should be an opportunity for each community of Christians to face the injustices within its own group, injustices which the real bourgeois society frequently accepts in a blasé manner and simply as a matter of fact.

One could also re-formulate an utterance from the Sermon on the Mount (Mt. 5, 23 ff.) as follows:

> When you therefore enter the confessional and there you remember that your brother has something against you, then go first to him and reconcile yourself with your brother; then come and receive the word of forgiveness of God and of the Church, which is true and real only when your brother has first forgiven you.

The old penitential practice with its long and harsh periods of contrition before the sinner was again reconciled to the Church and thereby to God, shows that formerly the Church had a very clear awareness of the fact that the sacramental word of absolution could not replace the inner, authentic and very real turning away from guilt, working itself out in the penitent, but rather that it rested upon it as an unconditional prerequisite.

The "penance" which the priest in the sacrament of penance lays upon the confessing sinner can be nothing but a small sign of the fact that a willingness must exist to strive for that inner and concrete conversion, without which all "confessing" remains only empty ritualism, and with which an unconverted heart would vainly try to fortify itself against God.

A second consideration is also important. Even though the grievous act of guilt must be made known in the sacrament, the sacramental confession is in its ultimate meaning an ever-renewed self-surrender of the total person to the merciful grace of God; of the person who, in the "judgment" of this sacrament, surrenders himself unconditionally to the mercy of God with all his opaque past, present and incalculable future, because he does not want to judge himself nor justify himself before God, but rather to let true justice be promised and granted to him as the mercy of God. Hence all scrupulousness in the examination of the individual sins, their precise listing, etc., would be a sign that one has not understood the true significance of this sacrament which, in its last analysis, is not a question of sins but rather of a sinful man who is encompassed by God's mercy and who can grasp, who can accept, historically and socially, this situation in the word of forgiveness of the Church, coming from God, and superabundantly overcoming all his guilt.

Traditional theology has expended a great deal of needless energy to distinguish between complete contrition on the basis of the love of God and an incomplete contrition, which no doubt acquires an authentic distance from guilt based on motives of faith, but is not yet real love, only something moving toward it. This distinction may be theoretically correct. But it does not have much importance in actual practice. For whoever is really capable of turning away from guilt, whoever no longer culpably absolutizes a finite good, for such a person the real difficulty of loving God no longer exists; for, just as the heart of man cannot contain the fullness of its own love but must be ever-giving; so, too, the love of God which man is constantly receiving and by which man lives, is constantly giving Itself to man.

In practice these two theoretically distinguishable kinds of contrition coexist, though one or the other may emerge more strongly in our consciousness at a particular time.

The dark mystery of guilt as a threatening possibility or as a reality in our life is never wholly overcome in our always ongoing history. We would be denying the ultimate dignity and significance of our life and of the Gospel were we to conduct ourselves as though we had nothing else to do but to attend to matters knowledgeably and soberly so that we might live with bourgeois ease, unthreatened by the police and enjoying every moment of our life.

Our life is the history of an ultimate freedom before God and thus is always threatened by true guilt. It may happen to us in particular situations or even in our old age that the final goodness of our freedom becomes for us a matter of disturbing and threatening importance. But in the last analysis we remain persons who must flee from ourselves and from the dark mystery of our threatening guilt in order to find our true selves in God. Whoever has understood the importance of this flight, this critical distancing of ourselves from ourselves and from this or that incident in us and in our life, whoever has understood this knows that it comes about only by allowing oneself to be loved by an infinite and all-forgiving love, which is called God, and by believing, hoping and loving in this love. For such a person the flight to God's word of forgiveness, which is most distinctly spoken through the word of Jesus in the Church, is not a matter of panic or of coming apart at the seams or of being insecure about life, but rather of a liberating experience achieved through God Himself.

We can try to suppress our guilt in the banality of a mere sober and reasonable life lived without illusions. In the long run this attempt is doomed to failure. There then exists only a two-fold possibility: to remain incarcerated in the hopelessness of our guilt or to have the courage to let our guilt be forgiven through that mystery of incomprehensibility, which we call God.

Christianity is this message: we should allow ourselves to be forgiven. And the Church offers us the means: the sacrament of penance.

Translated by Salvator Attanasio

5

ORDERS

Vessels of Clay

As the people redeemed in Jesus Christ, we offer the sacrifice of the new covenant on the altars of our Church. More than this we cannot do, even on the most special occasions. For there is no greater deed than this, and there is no way in which its value can really be increased: the Lord of ages becomes present in our midst—He who is the heart of the world, and whose act of love moves the stars and takes up everything with Him into the glory of God.

And yet on the day of a priest's first Mass we do offer the everlasting thanksgiving prayer in a special way. For we celebrate the hour when a man, consecrated to be a priest of Jesus Christ, performs for the first time that act which in a noble, Godlike monotony he is to perform every day for the rest of his life, until his life is finally consumed in that sacrifice that he daily celebrates and in whose acceptance alone all earthly reality sees itself accepted before the infinite majesty of God.

Why do we celebrate such a day? Does the Church invite Her faithful to make a kind of first installment of the laurels to a young man who has not yet done anything else but offer God his heart and his life, when actually it is only the completed sacrifice that ought to be celebrated? No, we are not honoring any man. We are honoring only the priesthood of

Jesus Christ. We are honoring the Church, the entire Church of all those redeemed, made holy, and called to eternal life. We are honoring Her to whom we all belong, whether we are priests or "merely" believers and sanctified. For we are all knit so closely into one body that the grace, dignity, or power that comes to one man graces and lifts all the others, and in one man's being called to service we glimpse the holy dignity of all.

Taken from among Men

When Paul in the Epistle to the Hebrews speaks of the priest, the first thing he says is that he is taken from among men. So much so that even the eternal high priest Jesus Christ wanted to be born of a woman, subject to the Law, a pilgrim through the valley of this transitory world, the Son of Man, a man, making himself like us in everything. The priest is a man. He is not made from another kind of clay than the rest of us. He is your brother. He continues to share the lot of man after the hand of God has rested on him in the form of the bishop's hand. The lot of the weak and the weary, the lot of the discouraged, the unsuccessful, and the sinner.

But men are offended when someone appears to do God's business and still is only a man. They want messengers who speak more brilliantly, heralds who preach more persuasively, hearts that burn with a hotter flame. They would gladly receive God's representative, provided he always had the upper hand, had an answer for everything, could handle every problem. But what is the terrible and happy truth? Those who come are weak men, who live in fear and trembling, men who themselves must pray over and over, "Lord, I believe, help my unbelief!" men who themselves must keep beating their breast, "Lord, be merciful to me, a sinner!"

And still they preach the faith that conquers the world and bring the grace that makes redeemed saints out of lost sinners. God sends men. They come and through their poor humanity they say, "Look, it is the likes of us that God takes pity on. Look, the star of grace has risen for the poor and the stupid, the desperate and the dying." As the human messengers of the everlasting God, they say, "Do not be scandalized at us. We know that we carry God's treasure in vessels of clay; we know that our shadow keeps darkening God's light, which we ought to bring to you. Be merciful towards us; do not judge us; feel sympathy with us weaklings, on whose shoulders God has loaded more grace than we can carry. You can take this as a promise for yourselves, the fact that we too are men. From it learn that God has no horror of human beings. You will someday feel horror and be shocked at yourselves, when you experience in yourselves what man is and what is in man. Blessed will you be then, those of you who have not been scandalized at the man in the priest. He is human so that you can believe that man—poor, real man—can possess the grace of God."

Messenger of God's Truth

There is something at once weird and blessed about God's truth. It is quite simple and does not make such rapid progress as the truth of men—who have been clever enough to succeed in inventing an atom bomb. God's truth may slip into men's hearts without their knowing it; it may seem to be there only in a little piece, for example in silent humility of heart, in a nameless longing of the mind, in the resignation with which a man accepts the silent dispositions of Fate in spite of her refusal to justify them.

But tiny as it is, when it is there in the power of the Holy Spirit of God, then it is wholly there, and in it the beginning of love and eternal life. But this plain and single truth of God, in which God speaks himself into the inmost heart of man, is the truth that is present in the world because it flowed out of the pierced heart of the Christ of God. And hence this truth wants to be made flesh in human words, wants to enter into

all men's thoughts and words, wants to become the uninter-
rupted theme of an endless symphony which peals through
every hall of the universe. This truth wants to be explained
and preached, wants to slip through the portals of the ears
into men's hearts, and out of the private chamber of their
hearts, to mount up and penetrate into every area of man's
activity, be preached from the rooftops, judging and purifying, redeeming and filling, and weave itself together with the
whole of human truth.

And this is why this truth has its messengers, human messengers. They speak a human word. But it is filled with divine
truth. And what they say is very, very old, still not yet
grasped; they say the truth—which is the only thing that
never fades, never wears out, never gets used up. They say
God—God of eternal majesty, God of eternal life; they say
that God Himself is our life; they call out that death is not the
end, that the world's cleverness is foolishness and shortsightedness, that there is a judgment, a justice, and an everlasting
life. They always say the same thing. Monotonous to the nth
degree. They say it to themselves and to others; for both have
to confess that neither has as yet grasped what is being
preached—God, the living God, the true God, the God who
has revealed Himself, God the father of our Lord Jesus Christ,
God, who with shameless prodigality pours His own infinity
into our heart without our noticing it, God, who turns our
hellish transitoriness into the dawn of eternal life—and we
are unwilling to believe it. That is what these messengers say.
That is what they have studied and meditated over, and strug-
gled, sometimes desperately, to put into the small mind and
narrow heart which is themselves. And they have not finished
their task. They are still God's apprentices. And yet God bids
them to speak about what they themselves have only half
grasped. So they begin. They stutter, they are embarrassed,
they realize that everything they have to say sounds so odd
and improbable on the lips of a mere man.

But they go and deliver the message. And the miracle happens: they actually find men who hear the word of God in this odd talk, men into whose heart the word penetrates, judging, redeeming, and making happy, consoling and dispensing strength in weakness, even though they say it, even though they deliver the message badly. But God is with them. With them in spite of their misery and sinfulness. They preach not themselves but Jesus Christ, they preach in His name. To the marrow of their bones they are ashamed that He said, "Whoever hears you, hears me; whoever despises you, despises me." But He said it. And so they go and deliver the message. They know that it is possible to be sounding brass and tinkling cymbal and to be oneself lost after having preached to others. But they have not chosen themselves. They were called and sent. And so they have to go and preach. In season and out. They traverse the fields of the world and scatter the seed of God. They are thankful when a little of it grows. And they implore the mercy of God for themselves, so that not too much of it remains unfruitful through their fault. They sow in tears. And usually it is someone else who reaps what they have sowed. But they know this: the word of God must run and bring fruit; for it is God's blessed truth, heart's light, comfort in death, and hope of eternal life.

Dispenser of the Divine Mysteries

The word that God put in the mouth of the priest is not just a word-in-general, spoken out into the indeterminate. It is God's word; hence it ought to find its mark in the individual in his uniqueness and in his unique place in time. It ought to be said to the individual—in the morning hours of his life, when he begins to create an eternity in time; on the many everydays of his pilgrimage, during which he has to pick his way laboriously through all the valleys and meanderings of a human life; in the dead despair of guilt; in that holy moment, the moment of death, when it looks as though the fruits of time will issue once and for all into the inescapable grasp of death and eternity. In such moments must the priest speak the word of God, the mighty and creative word, the word that does not talk but acts, the sacramental word. *I baptize thee, I absolve thee from thy sins, this is my body*—such are the words, spoken in the person of Christ, which the priest speaks into man's concrete situation.

And what they proclaim they bring along with them; what they announce they effect, since they are God's words. In virtue of these words the priest is completely stripped of power and completely powerful, because they are not his words any more at all, and they are wholly the words of Christ. But he is allowed to say them. To say them over and over. To say them patiently, believingly, indefatigably. All other words that he uses, what he says in preaching and instructions, are only an echo, an explanation, a commentary added to these basic words of his priestly existence which he speaks in the administration of the sacraments, where he accompanies them with holy actions that use the poor elements of earth to hide the bliss of heaven, fecundating them with Christ's word.

Thus graced with Christ's efficacious word, he confers Christ's mysteries, the sacraments. Men usually want something else from him: bread, the solution of the social question, recipes for being happy on this earth. They are irritated and bored when they hear over and over only words that have to be *believed*, that only produce results in God's eternity, that have no value in the traffic of the markets of the world. The priest, however, goes on speaking his word, the word of the sacraments. What they produce cannot be tested in the laboratories of men, who want to recognize as real only what they find there. But it works. And so at his word the fortunes of the children of God take their beginning, sins are forgiven, the banquet of everlasting life is celebrated, there wells up out of the murky depths of death the light that is never extinguished.

With the gifts, I should say the offer, of God's mysteries, the priest, like a man from another world, stands on the street corners while the endless procession of men and their histories hurries by, speeding towards death or towards life, one cannot say which. Whoever pauses, whoever accepts the offer of this wanderer between two worlds who is the priest, that man receives the secrets of God; in time he finds eternity, in death life, in darkness light and the pure presence of God. And the man who is authorized to speak into the ever unique situation of the individual these words of the living God's sacramental presence and efficaciousness in the holy Church, that man we call the priest.

Entrusted with the Sacrifice

Once we have begun to speak of the priest's work in the world, we must consider more expressly than we have yet done the mystery that is comparable to the heart in the body of the Church, inasmuch as it conducts with even pulse beats the nourishing strength of the blood to the individual members. The priest is the man to whom the sacrifice of the Church, the liturgical repetition of Christ's Last Supper, is committed, and because this is after all the inmost and ultimate thing in the priestly existence, we celebrate the beginning of that kind of life, not with his first baptism or with the first time he says the words of forgiveness of sin, but with the first time he celebrates the sacrifice of the altar, and we celebrate it with him.

Here at such a moment we find everything brought together: men, the Church, God, Christ, the sacrifice of the cross, the living and the dead, the poverty of earth and the blessings of heaven. For here is the glorified Lord in the midst of His community, the community of the sanctified and redeemed, whom the priest, commissioned by Christ Himself and possessing an authority that comes from above and not from below, leads in before the throne of grace, so that this community offers the eternal Father as the sacrifice of this entire Church the Lord made present by the priest's word, to the praise of His name and the salvation of all who celebrate this sacrifice and whom we remember in love in fidelity. Authorized by Christ himself, who loves His Church and has given her His own sacrifice the priest has the power to celebrate the sacrifice of eternal reconciliation in the name of all, with all, and for all.

And if in this vocation he is supremely elevated by God above all others, then he is also supremely consumed and swallowed up by the flames of his pure service before God on behalf of mankind. At this time he is allowed to carry the Lord's body and to grasp the chalice of salvation, which is filled with the world's ransom—not in order to exalt himself, the priest, but in order to bring salvation to the whole people of God. What he does surrounded by happy friends on the day of his first solemn Mass, he will do every day of his life. Every day in youth and old age, on the gray mornings that begin the daily grind and at the terrible moments that find their way into every life. And each time this poor little celebration will hold the content of all the riddles of existence, and the solution of all the riddles: the body which was handed over and the blood which was spilt for the forgiveness of sin. Everything will be contained together in this short half hour every day; for here we have present as Victim and as Conqueror the one who is in Himself the real union of the riddle with its solution, the union of earth with heaven, the union of man with God, in the celebration of that one instant in which on the cross the greatest distance between the two became the inseparable nearness.

The priest is man, messenger of God's truth, dispenser of the divine mysteries, one who makes Christ's single sacrifice present again. What great good fortune! Of course every man has his calling from God, his fortune decided for him from eternity, his commission too in the body of Christ which is the Church. A purely profane existence cannot be found; nobody has one. But the reality of God, which for most men appears most exclusively in the depths of their inmost conscience and in the silent secrecy of their private life, that reality, under the call of God to the priest, forces its way up out of the depths and floods every reach of his life. All of it must be consumed by God or pressed into His own glorious but demanding service.

This is the life of the priest: to dwell completely in the explicit nearness of God. A life at once happy and terrifying. Happy, because God alone is happiness; terrifying, because man finds it difficult to survive in the midst of this frightening splendor of God. No wonder then that the noblest plant is always the most fragile too! No wonder that the high calling conceals within it the danger of the greatest falls—the danger that the priest will think he does not need to be a man any more, the danger of being unsympathetic towards other men, of letting his human side wither away, the danger of flight away from God into the more familiar company of men, the danger of the pitiful compromise, of the attempt to meet the superhuman demands of the priestly life by cheap mediocrity.

When someone dares to take up the happy and terrifying life of a priest, then the happy occasion can strike us speechless with fear, because here is the beginning of something that no human being can finish. But we comfort ourselves with the grace of God; not we but that grace will finish what it has begun. For He who called the priest is true to His word and His graces are given without repentance. But during this celebration of the holy sacrifice let us pray for the Church on earth: pray God to send workers into His harvest, for the workers are few. Pray for our priests, that they begin in the fear and joy of the Lord and persevere in faithful service up to that happy end which all aspire to, when all vocations will find one happy end in the endless sacrificial celebration of eternity, when the Son and we with Him give over everything to the Father, so that God may be all in all. Amen.

Translated by James M. Quigley, S.J.

6

MATRIMONY

Trusting and Loving

"This is a great mystery, and I mean in reference to Christ and the Church."

(Eph. 5,32)

This is what Paul says about the loving union of a man and woman in marriage. This hour belongs to that great mystery. For today, before the altar of God, and with the blessing of Christ and His Church, we see the beginning of a new life, a life of love and faithfulness. This holy adventure of marriage is seen, even from the human point of view, to be part of the mystery of God.

When a man, in the existential awareness of his own being, freely disposes of his life, when he dares to entrust his heart, his life, his destiny and the eternal worth of his own person to another human being, thus abandoning himself to the strange, unknown and impenetrable mystery of another personality (and this is possible only in the supreme adventure of love and trust), then such an experience—which, seen by others, may appear insignificant, almost banal, because it occurs so frequently—is indeed what it appears to the lovers themselves to be: the unique miracle of love.

This is an experience which partakes of the divine, for it

involves the whole man and his whole destiny. When a marriage is freely contracted, the man and wife, whether they are aware of it or not, enter the presence of God. There is always a silent Companion, perhaps never given a name, who embraces, preserves, redeems and blesses all: we call Him God. Such an experience is boundless because it leads to what is infinite and unconditional, and is possible only in the infinite dimension of a spiritual person, reaching out to God. There is always something free and boundless in a truly personal love which is superior to all the chances and changes of life, so that when a man and woman truly love each other they grow beyond themselves and enter a stream which flows into infinity.

That which dwells in the infinite distance, and which is silently evoked in such a love, can finally be called by one name only: God. In Him is the assurance of eternal love; He is the guardian of the dignity of the person who lovingly entrusts himself to another fallible and finite person; He is the fulfillment of the infinite promise of love, which love would not be capable of honoring if it had to find this fulfillment in itself alone. He is the unfathomable depth (in grace) of the other human being without which, in the end, every man would be empty and meaningless for all others. He is the endless distance which a lover enters to find room to lay down the burdens which he will not let his loved one bear, but which, borne by him alone, would crush him. For both, He is true forgiveness, beyond and above all human forgiveness, without which no love can last for long. He is holy fidelity in person, and each must be true to Him in order to be true forever to the other. In a word, He is love itself, the source of all other loves, and this must be open to Him if they are not to be merely dangerous experiences, blindly entered into, which founder in their own infinite hazards.

But the message of the Christian Catholic faith is that marriage shares in the mystery of God in an even more profound sense than that which we learn from the unconditional character of human love. Marriage, says the Church, is a sacrament. This is easily said, but we must understand what is meant by these words in order to comprehend the almost terrifying audacity with which we affirm such a sublime thing about a human action that is apparently so commonplace.

For Christians, marriage is a sacrament and therefore conveys grace. But this grace is not only the assistance God gives a married pair in order to help them to be loving, true, patient and brave, unselfish and ready to bear each other's burdens. Grace is not merely God's help in the performance of those duties and obligations which everyone in this world recognizes and, at least in theory, accepts. Grace is more than this: it means divine life, eternal power, a share in the divine nature, a pledge of future blessedness, a seal and an anointing, the beginning and foundation of a life which, grafted on God's own life, is worth living forever and ever. Grace is in truth God Himself who, in the infinite perfection of His life and of His unimaginable glory, wishes to give Himself to His own spiritual creature. It is true that all this is still hidden under the veil of faith and hope, still incomprehensible and mysterious; it may not yet have arisen from the profoundest depths of our soul to the surface of our daily experience. But all this, which we call divine grace, exists and it is this which God, in the innermost depths of our being, inaccessible even to ourselves, has sowed as the seed of eternal life, of freedom and blessed truth. This is what we call by a sober little word: grace.

We may say of this grace, and of this alone, which is not merely an everyday help from God to enable us to be morally good, that it is increased through the sacrament of marriage.

This means that wherever Christians marry, wherever in this world is raised the standard of indissoluble love, which is an image of the redeeming love of Christ for His Church, there grace is present. The divine life is present, unless the mortal sin of the lovers has frustrated it, and they begin a new and more profound dynamic experience which, through the operation of the Holy Spirit, may lead these two persons further and deeper into the life of God Himself. New depths of divine splendor will be revealed in that spiritual sphere in which God gives Himself to be the life of a man's soul. In Christian marriage there grows to sweeter tenderness and stronger loyalty that love which binds man to his God, and the unique mystery of all life becomes ever more profound and more alive, more powerful and all-embracing than before: the mystery of the discovery of God in the intimacy of His communion with the soul of man.

These are the daring and sublime assertions we make about marriage when we say that it is a sacrament. So we may affirm that it is not only a loving communion between two persons, but therefore and thereby a communion through grace with God Himself. There is no doubt that this experience cannot be realized without the free inner consent of these two human beings, and that the lovers become aware of this truth only insofar as they open their hearts to it with faith and love. Nevertheless, it is certain that the experience of this grace begins today, and it can lead to this union with God.

That is why marriage is truly a divine mystery, a part of the liturgy in which the mysteries of eternity are here present with us during a sacred celebration, and are bearers of salvation.

Marriage is intended to be fruitful, fruitful in every sphere and dimension of human life.

It is intended to give us strength and courage in our daily lives, because two creatures will now share their burdens with each other, according to the words of the Apostle: "Bear one another's burdens, for by so doing you will fulfill the law of Christ."

Marriage should also be spiritually fruitful. Since love is the source of wisdom, then the wisdom of those lovers who are lawfully joined for life must be great indeed. Such wisdom may be simple and concealed, but it is the experience of love itself. There are many who wish to gather this knowledge from the Tree of Life, but their love is not true because they are not faithful. They shun the suffering which love entails because they confuse love with caprice, with infatuation, with that purely animal passion by means of which nature achieves her end. But whoever truly loves knows what love is. And only those who have known it can understand that God Himself is love. For what can we hope to know if we have no notion of who He is, the incomprehensible, the holy mystery which enfolds us and in which we find in all our doing our daily, life-long experience of the painful inexpressibility of love?

Love must be fruitful in children. Marriage accepts this possibility, uncalculated and unplanned: it accepts it from the living God, the Father who also, from all eternity, begets the Son in His own image and loves and is loved by Him in the Holy Spirit.

That children should be born of a marriage is a commonplace in this world, and yet this commonplace is an extraordinary thing. We all hope that some part of our lives may endure and become eternal; we hope to draw from time's press the wine of eternal joy. But in the fruitfulness of marriage, eternity is realized in such a way that we do not know whether to raise a holy hymn of praise in exultation of this sublime human possibility, or be frightened to death by the fear of what a man can do, almost without thought.

A new person is born. But this means a new reality which will never end and will always be itself: a life and a destiny have begun which will last forever, and can never be wiped out. What begins in this way certainly continues as the life of an individual, who acts for himself and leaves his father and his mother to become a new person, so that even his parents can no longer understand this free and original being unless they love him with that love that teaches them not to seek themselves in others, but only the reality of those other beings. Nevertheless, the fact remains that the parents have given birth to something eternal which will never come to an end and can never be altered or recalled. A new human being is a new eternity in God's sight.

To give birth to an eternal being is something which requires authorization from God: we can find the courage only when we receive His blessing. No wonder then that men who shun God shun also the thought of having children. But Christian marriage may and must give birth to new eternal life. In fact, the infinite God gives Himself unendingly to the being we call man, because God revealed Himself as man in His Incarnate Word. And He, the source of all fatherhood in heaven and earth, continues the adventure of His generous love through the action of the parents, whose love becomes fruitful in new life.

At this moment something great is happening. May God bestow His blessing on it so that it may turn to good! What is now beginning has begun countless times before, and God alone knows whether the result was good or bad. And yet, in a sense, what is beginning today has never happened before. For everyone's life, and therefore everyone's marriage, is unique, so unique that the man who lives a married life, and in so doing wins eternal life, has indeed deserved to live forever.

Today there begins something new that has never happened before. What must be experienced here has never been experienced before. This may be said of every marriage, but it is nonetheless true. It may be said of every person that he is unique, but this does not make any individual less unique. And the same is true of marriage, of every marriage. Certainly many counsels and much good advice, inspired by human experience and the heavenly wisdom of the Church, may be offered about the way to be followed, but the unique mystery to which the unique marriage leads is known only to God. And therefore the wisdom of men and of the Church must here keep silence. We can only say: "Go with God, He alone knows all. May the Lord be with you! May He be your light and strength, your mutual loyalty and the eternal source of your love! Go with Him, go together; together and with Him follow all the paths of this life, so that you may be led into His unspeakable glory."

We are all riddles, even to ourselves. Therefore marriage and love also are mysteries which can only be resolved in the greater mystery of God. If you have placed your trust in Him, the mystery of marriage, the great mystery of which Paul speaks, will be full of meaning and power, full of everlasting salvation.

In any case there begins here today the mystery of a unity which did not exist before. It is worth experiencing: indeed it should reflect the splendor of God in a way that can only be shown in this unique life shared in common, in the midst of this finite world. And that is why the experience of life, which you have now begun, is, through all the vicissitudes and perils of your lives, one single and unique experience which will enable you to know God Himself in a unique way.

We have already said that the unique experience now beginning must remain a mystery, so how is it possible to give counsels and directions about the way which must be followed, this first and last time? Perhaps it is best to repeat what Scripture has already said, for these admonitions are as fresh now as they were when the Holy Spirit first uttered them through human lips:

> Husbands, love your wives, as Christ loved the Church and gave Himself up for Her, that He might sanctify Her, having cleansed Her by the washing of water with the Word, that He might present the Church to Himself in splendor, without spot or wrinkle or any such thing, that She might be holy and without blemish. Even so husbands should love their wives as their own bodies. He who loves his wife loves himself (Eph. 5:25–28).

Put on then, as God's chosen ones, holy and beloved, compassion, kindness, lowliness, meekness and patience, forbearing one another and, if one has a complaint against another, forgiving each other; as the Lord has forgiven you, so you also must forgive. And above all these put on love, which binds everything together in perfect harmony (Col. 3:12–14).

Never flag in zeal, be aglow with the Spirit, serve the Lord. Rejoice in your hope, be patient in tribulation, be constant in prayer. Contribute to the needs of the saints, practice hospitality. Bless those who persecute you; bless and do not curse them. Rejoice with those who rejoice, weep with those who weep. Live in harmony with one another; do not be haughty, but associate with the lowly; never be conceited. Repay no one evil for evil, but take thought for what is noble in the sight of all. If possible, so far as it depends upon you, live peaceably with all (Rom. 12:11–18).

And whatever you do, in word or deed, do everything in the name of the Lord Jesus, giving thanks to God the Father through Him (Col. 3:17).

Rejoice in the Lord always; again I will say, rejoice. Let all men know your forbearance. The Lord is at hand. Have no anxiety about anything, but in everything by prayer and supplication with thanksgiving let your requests be made known to God. And the peace of God, which passes all understanding, will keep your hearts and minds in Christ Jesus (Phil. 4:4–7).

Let marriage be held in honor among all, and let the marriage bed be undefiled; for God will judge the immoral and adulterous (Heb. 13:4).

Likewise you wives, be submissive to your husbands, so that some, though they do not obey the word, may be won without a word by the behavior of their wives (I Pet. 3:1).

. . . that you may be blameless and innocent, children of God without blemish in the midst of a crooked and perverse generation, among whom you shine as lights in the world (Phil. 2:15).

You men, love your wives, and be not angered against them (Col. 3:18).

Love is patient and kind; love is not jealous or boastful; it is not arrogant or rude. Love does not insist on its own way; it is not irritable or resentful; it does not rejoice in wrong, but rejoices in the right. Love bears all things, believes all things, hopes all things, endures all things . . . So faith, hope, love abide, these three; but the greatest of these is love. Make love your aim (I Cor. 13:4–7; 13).

May the God of peace Himself sanctify you wholly; and may your spirit and soul and body be kept sound and blameless at the coming of our Lord Jesus Christ. He who calls you is faithful, and He will do it (I Thess. 5:23, 24).

The liturgy of this nuptial consent finds its fulfillment in the celebration of the holy sacrifice of the Mass. And this is as it should be. The grace of matrimony is the grace of Christ, and therefore comes from the source of all grace: the pierced heart of the Redeemer who upon the altar of the Cross sacrificed Himself for His Bride, the Church, and allowed Himself to sink into the infinite darkness of death, trusting that thus and by this means He would consign His spirit into His Father's hands, as with holy generous love He gave His life for the salvation of all. All grace comes from the pierced heart of Christ. And so it is also with the grace of marriage, without which no union can be preserved and blessed.

Therefore the grace of marriage also bears the marks of its origin; it is the grace of self-sacrificing love, of the love which gives itself and endures and forgives, selfless love which hides its pain; it is the grace of love which is faithful until death, which bears the fruit of new life, and survives death; it is the grace of the love which St. Paul praised, love that is kind, that believes all, bears all, hopes all and suffers all, love that never ends, without which everything else is worthless.

When here and now, in the holy ceremony before the sacred altar of God, we mingle the celebration of such a nuptial bond with the celebration of the supreme act of the self-sacrificing love of Christ for His Church, what we do is in itself a prayer and signifies the heart's acceptance of such a love.

The God who has called you is faithful and will bring all things to perfection, says St. Paul about growth in Christian faith. So every sacrament, including this which is here celebrated, is in truth a moment in this Christian growth in grace.

Therefore we may here apply these words of the Apostle, trusting in the power of grace and of the divine promise in all that begins here today. He is faithful who has called you and He will perfect your love.

But the perfection, the supreme fulfillment of the love which today pledges eternal fidelity, is found where every human life finds its perfection: through Jesus Christ and the blessed power of His grace, in God to whom be glory now, and from everlasting to everlasting, when all things shall be brought to perfection.   Amen.

Translated by Dorothy White

7

THE ANOINTING
OF THE SICK

Saving and Healing

Certain critical situations in a man's life may not at first sight appear to be spiritual experiences. But they become part of the history of his salvation as soon as they force him to come to a true and integral understanding of his whole life, to see it either as nonsense or as a dark mystery, in which infinite love draws ever nearer to him, saving, forgiving, freeing and redeeming him, enabling him to share in the divine nature. A really grave illness is an experience of this sort.

By illness in this sense we do not mean every ailment which may cause us pain or make us turn for help to a doctor, or even to a hospital. There are some illnesses in the modern medical sense of the word which, however unpleasant and costly in terms of time and money, nevertheless from their onset are, or at least seem to be, under the control of the sick man himself and of his doctor: slight ailments for which nature, with man's help, can find a remedy and a cure, and which merely prove to him that he is still alive and fundamentally healthy. But there are other illnesses which, even when a man may hope to survive them, are messengers and portents of death; they reveal the essential precariousness of our mortal life; they bring us face to face with our own mortal destiny, with that fear of death and longing for death which, although they may be suppressed, secretly rule our lives. They make us feel imperiled to the very core of our being; we are alone and helpless. They are experiences of imminent death even when, as we have said, the struggle between death and life is not yet decided and there is still reason for hope. Modern medicine may succeed in keeping such an illness at bay until the last moments of life, almost until that moment when life finally plunges into death and a man begins to lose his power of speech in the unavoidable solitude of death, so that he can give us no further sign of what he feels in his utter prostration.

Illnesses of this type produce a stark awareness of ourselves, of our utter helplessness and our unavoidable end. Why do we refuse to accept this? Why do we shun this experience? Why, when such an illness overpowers us, do we not see ourselves in all our nakedness and need? Why do we not have the courage to admit our mortality not only theoretically ("All men must die: I suppose even I must one day die"), but also to realize that actually we are all dying men? This truth may be realized even during a grave illness from which we recover, when we struggle bravely, but in a spirit of detachment, against death. When instead we play hide-and-seek with a grave illness, do we not forfeit the supreme dignity of man, that of knowing who he is, wholly and in all truth, and so of accepting him as he is, as a man who will be torn apart in death and can then truly find himself only in a final supreme acceptance of the worst pangs of dissolution? Illness is an experience which brings us wholly face to face with ourselves, and therefore it is part of the history of our salvation.

But is a man capable of passing this test? It is the peculiar characteristic of illness that on the one hand it places a man in a most critical situation in which he is called upon to make the final supreme decision (that of abandoning himself to a Will which he cannot understand but which he believes is working for his salvation and is worthy of his trust), and on the other hand it leaves him weak, failing, foolish, worn out, tired and empty. Nor must we forget that we can never know for sure in which moment of life we shall bring ourselves to give our fearless consent to our final destiny. It need not necessarily be the moment which the doctor calls death. The real act of death may take place before physical death has occurred, in a sublime experience of love, trust and awareness, a moment in which a man overcomes his fears and abandons himself utterly to the supreme Mystery of his existence. But in any case, serious illness is in itself such a situation, a mysterious and doubly dangerous crisis in which a man is called upon to make the supreme gesture of his whole life while at the same time he is reduced to the last stage of weakness.

How can he pass this test? Only in the grace of God can he find the strength to overcome—the grace of God who has brought about this situation in order to reveal His mysterious purpose and to show the Lord's death and His love, the grace of God who alone rules the destinies of men. Christians know that the obedience and generous love which were shown in the dark hour of the physical death of Jesus, and on no other occasion, are for them the source of salvation and of sanctifying grace. Therefore Christians believe also that, for followers of Jesus, death is the supreme test of faith, and that this test can only be overcome by faith in the grace of the One who knew how to die, Jesus of Nazareth.

This is true also of the situation of the sick when death is visibly near. It is now that they need the grace of God because it enables them to accept their situation obediently, accepting alike the necessity for a supreme decision and their own powerlessness (theologians call this effectual, actual grace). They need it because, in this fearful plunge into an abyss far below all the earlier certainties and stabilities characteristic of our daily life, down into the unfathomable depths of an inscrutable and inexorable Will, the grace of Christ interprets for us the saving mystery of love which forgives and sanctifies. (Theologians would here refer to the existence, growth and operation of sanctifying grace.)

The thought of imminent death and of its agony casts us into a merciless solitude in which we are left alone to deal with ourselves and with God. A man's responsibility for himself, for his own freedom and for his docile acceptance of the inevitability of his fate, is part of his very nature and cannot and must not be taken away from him. And in grave illness this responsibility acquires a dread and unavoidable significance which all must face alone. No one may attempt to spare himself or others such a confrontation—and in any case this would be impossible.

But this is only one aspect of the whole truth. Even in his utter solitude a man is not alone: God is with him. As the old Israelites used to say, He is by the bedside of the sick. And the sick man has with him also the blessed community of all believers, of all who love and pray, who while they live try to practice obedience unto death and to look with faith upon the dying Christ—upon Him whom their sins have wounded, upon Him who will send to every one of them the angel of life and death. And since this holy community, which we call the Church, draws its life from the Lord's death, so the dying man, although alone, is never forsaken by his brethren.

Even the most out-of-the-way, solitary death is the fruit of the deaths of all who live and die in Christ, and salvation—although proper to him and inalienable—comes to the dying man in union with those who, by virtue of Christ's saving love, have become the saving community of the Church, in which he has a part insofar as he accepts with faith, hope and love his own solitary death, and receives the grace to accept it as a gift from God who thus reveals Himself, the God from whom the Church draws Her life.

In fact, although unseen, the holy people of God are there in prayer around the loneliest sufferer. And if one of the holy community, even at the last moment and in silence, is present at the bedside of the sick man, whether he be related to him or not (a member of the Church, a doctor, or a priest), then the eternal truth becomes manifest that we die in Christ, and are therefore always within His mysterious Body, which is the Church.

We are now perhaps a little more prepared to understand the words from the fifth chapter of the letter of St. James[1] and to appreciate their deeper meaning:

> Is any among you sick? Let him call for the elders of the Church, and let them pray over him, anointing him with oil in the name of the Lord; and the prayer of faith will save the sick man, and the lord will raise him up; and if he has committed sins, he will be forgiven. Therefore confess your sins to one another, and pray for one another, that you may be healed. The prayer of a righteous man has great power in its effects.

In this brief meditation there is no room for learned exegesis. But even without it the text is clear. St. James is speaking of illness and of its theological significance, to which we have already referred: grave illness and the danger of death, which —one must again point out—need not imply the certainty of death, but signifies what is, from the medical point of view, an incurable condition. Otherwise the sick man would surely not have caused the elders of the community the trouble of coming to him—he would have gone himself to them.

The elders are the leaders of the Christian community,[2] those who by divine calling and by the laying on of hands are appointed to be the lawful pastors of a Christian Church, and who therefore may act with the special powers bestowed upon them "in the name of the Lord," the only head of the community. The fact that here a number of elders are referred to in one community reflects the conditions of the primitive Church.[3] Since the Church's constitution has assumed a monarchical form, the community has generally been represented by one priest. (Nevertheless, in the Eastern liturgies of the Catholic Church it is still possible and customary for several priests to be present at the rite of extreme unction.) What the Church does for the sick man is clearly described: a prayer full of faith is said "over" his sickbed and he is annointed with oil. The content and the purpose of this liturgical prayer, illustrated by the act of anointing, are for the healing of the sick man. This unction finds a precedent in late Jewish practice and the commandment Jesus gave to His apostles when He sent them into the country around Galilee.[4] This prayer is pronounced "in the name of the Lord," Jesus Christ, under His authority and by His command, and with the powers conferred by Him.

If we wish to understand more precisely the efficacy which James attributes (with no hint of any fear of failure on its part) to this liturgical prayer, we must now leave verse 15 in its apparent vagueness and reflect on the real essence of all Christian prayer.

A petition is a prayer, the appeal to God of a living man in a particular situation; he is right to implore God's help in overcoming a crisis in the way which, from his own point of view, seems most suitable, but at the same time he accepts his situation courageously and with the humility proper to a creature. Just as he asks for his daily bread (although hunger itself may be a grace) and for deliverance from evil (although a sunset might prove to be an eternal dawn), so in this present case he pleads that he may recover from his illness.

But prayer, in the Christian sense, is more than a wild cry of inner agony caused by physical distress, more than an appeal for deliverance, as he understands it: it is something more than the expression of a man's free choice. Prayer is true prayer only when it is directed to the unimaginable God and uttered in the name of Jesus, who by His death won life for Himself and for us. And so it is, in a mysterious unity which only the man who prays with faith can understand, an utter surrender to the inscrutable, sovereign, all-powerful will of God ("not my will but Thine be done") and a petition which, just because of this total surrender, is sure of being answered —it does not matter what earthly form God's answers take— since grace, which alone inspires the prayer, enshrines and preserves the creature's will in the will of One who is all power and love, and the infinitude of both. It is in this context of prayer, which James simply and naturally calls its "effects," that the granting of a petition must be understood: it always means the forgiveness of sin because all sickness, like death itself,[5] is a sign of sin, even when it is not the result of any fault on the part of the sick man.[6] In fact a true and perfect answer to prayer, conducive to salvation, is impossible without the forgiveness of sin. And it is also a healing and "raising up," which may consist in the actual recovery of health, granted by God in view of a more prolonged Christian preparation for final salvation or, in a mysterious but no less real sense, in a holy death in the Lord who is Himself our final health and salvation.

This prayer, together with the anointing recommended by James for the healing of the sick, was always used in Christian communities both in the East and in the West, although perhaps not so frequently as might have been expected, and sometimes in such a way that it was difficult to distinguish it from other liturgical acts. But the practice of anointing the infirm was always continued as a liturgical act of the Church.

In the most ancient liturgical books it is already implied in the rite of the consecration of oil for this purpose, and from the early Middle Ages onwards, together with confession and Holy Communion, it has been a permanent feature of the liturgy for the sick and dying. Since the 11th century it has been explicitly included as one of the seven sacraments, as is seen in the common profession of faith drawn up by the Eastern and Western churches at the Council of Lyon (1274) and at the Council of Florence (1439), and in answer to its rejection by the reformers of the 16th century, it was defined as a sacrament in the seventh Session (3–3–1547) and four-teenth Session (11–25–1551) of the Council of Trent.

The official doctrine of the Church on the anointing of the sick is very fully expounded in the doctrinal Decree of the fourteenth Session (1551) of the Council of Trent. We quote the most important passages:

The holy assembly of the Church has wished to follow up its teaching . . . about repentance by adding the following observations on the sacrament of Extreme Unction which, according to the doctrine of the Fathers of the Church, is not only the crowning act of the sacrament of penance but the crowning act of the whole Christian life, because this life must be a continual exercise of penitence . . . Our most merciful Redeemer has, so to speak, fortified the end of our life with a mighty rampart. In fact, even if our Enemy has throughout our lives always sought and seized every oppor-tunity to devour our souls,[7] yet he never tries so hard, employing all his deceitful wiles, to destroy us utterly and if possible to rob us of our faith in divine mercy, as in that moment in which he sees the end of our life drawing near.

This holy Unction of the sick was really and truly in-stituted by our Lord Jesus Christ as a sacrament of the New Covenant. It was referred to by Mark,[8] but it was James, the Lord's brother, who preached and commended it to the faithful. . . .[9] According to the apostolic tradition received by the Church, in these words he taught the matter, form, proper ministry and effect of this sacrament of salvation. In fact the Church has always understood the oil consecrated by the bishop to be its matter, and the Unction itself to be the most apt illustration of the grace of the Holy Spirit, with which the sick man's soul is invisibly anointed. The form of the sacrament is understood by the Church to be the words: "With this Unction . . . etc." The content and effect of this sacrament . . . is the grace of the Holy Spirit, whose Unction wipes away any sins that may still be unabsolved, with the consequences of sin, and raises up and strengthens the sick man's soul, arousing in him great confidence in the divine mercy. This confidence comforts him so that he may more easily bear the burden and pain of his illness, and more resolutely resist the temptations of Satan, who is always at his heels;[10] and sometimes, if the salvation of his soul requires it, he recovers also in bodily health.

Here may be added a paragraph about the anointing of the sick, from the Constitution *Lumen gentium* (no. 11) issued by Vatican II (1964), which throws further light on the symbolic meaning of the Unction.

> By means of the holy Unction of the sick, and the prayers of the priest, the Church entrusts the sick to the Lord, in order that He may comfort and save them; moreover, the Church exhorts the infirm to make their own contribution to the welfare of God's people by willingly offering their own sufferings in union with the Passion and death of Christ.

We do not intend here to explain definitely and precisely this doctrinal text. We leave it as it is. What may be said about it will be clear in the following observations, which on the basis of what has already been said, seek to offer a more systematic explanation of the doctrine of anointing the sick. We must therefore return to what we said at the beginning of our meditation, by way of introduction to the words of James.

In the language of theology and of piety we speak of grace —and yet we do not think much about it, and when we do, we imagine it to be a great mystery. It is indeed mysterious in that it is the supreme effort of human beings to understand the infinite mystery of God, and also the power to accept this blessed incapacity of ours to touch the foundation of our existence, to accept it and not to shun it in a cowardly manner in order to cling eagerly and anxiously to particular and finite power and pleasure, within the infinite horizon of our knowledge, our freedom and our activity. In short, grace is God

Himself insofar as, by dwelling in us, He shares with us His own infinitude by granting us forgiveness and life. Inasmuch as we, even in a vague and undefined way, become aware of this unfathomable mystery of our existence, and yet feel, even if we cannot explain it to ourselves, that this abyss leads to One whom we call God, the grace we receive is at one and the same time utterly mysterious and yet within our grasp because it is the incomprehensible foundation and fulfillment of our supreme experience.

Finally this indescribable and silent harmony at the very roots of our existence is experienced as something not external to our real life but deep within it, and naturally it is felt with particular intensity in our most intensely lived moments. That is why grace, and our awareness of it, have a wholly human character, and why the grace which is bestowed by the God-Man has the characteristics of an incarnation. It must therefore be particularly evident whenever, in the most critical events of human and Christian life, a man is brought starkly face to face with himself, and the dread but blessed mystery of his existence forces him to come to a decision.

One of these events is sickness. Naturally we cannot prevent it from taking hold of us. But we can try with all the means at our disposal to banish it to the extreme limits of our consciousness and to stifle its message in the dark recesses of our soul. This message is that we live precariously, that we have no final control over our destiny, and that we must obediently accept our own powerlessness. We cannot avoid this powerless condition: at the most we can only raise our cry of protest, subdued or clamorous, and offer our resistance— and this protest is the fundamental temptation of our whole life.

But if we accept what illness has to teach us, without necessarily despairing of recovery, then we become aware of grace: our own weakness becomes a gentle power of salvation, our void is mysteriously filled, our apparent abandonment to our fate becomes an unforeseeable victory.

The infinite extent of our willing acceptance of this experience, which embraces our whole life and then renounces it, is the operation of grace. Illness may be the occasion for the acceptance of this grace.

But on an occasion of this kind, when we see that illness is something which involves the whole man, we become aware of another aspect of faith: we are not alone. Naturally our loneliness during grave sickness oppresses us: the words of our relations and of our doctor sound dim and confused to our ears, like an incomprehensible murmur. Nevertheless, we are surrounded by the invisible and silent company of all who, in circumstances like our own, have accepted the will of God, of all who have found eternal life in this life and death of ours, and who have allowed themselves to be wholly absorbed into this mystery which softly and silently detaches us from ourselves (the mystery we usually call God).

When we feel united with the very source of our existence, then we are in the company of all those who have undergone this experience (theologically speaking, they are said to possess sanctifying grace). And it is true that every man is united with all others, and all others with him, in seeking that source of life which is salvation. We read in the Scriptures that if one member suffers, all suffer with him.

When we accept this experience of faith it is natural for us to wish that the community of the faithful who obediently accept the mystery (following Jesus, who was obedient unto death), the community we call the Church, should be visibly present at our bedside, so that the mysterious flow of divine life may not only circulate freely in us but may be seen, may become "incarnate" in the reality of our daily life. In this way grace, by means of this visible sign which it has created for itself, penetrates more deeply within us, and with its saving power sanctifies our living and dying.

This word, which gives a physical, incarnate form to the

hidden work of grace, is spoken by the Church through the mouth of Her appointed minister, and so transforms into a visible experience both the grace the sick man receives, with his own interior consent, and the grace of the Holy Church, filled with the spirit of God. In this word, grace is revealed and experienced, even while it assumes a form apprehensible to our bodily senses. So the revelation conveys the grace (and naturally the converse too is true: what is revealed and the mode of its revelation are indissoluble).

When the Church utters such a word of grace, illustrated and made more comprehensible by means of other gestures (washing, anointing, the laying on of hands, etc.) thus pledging the truth of Her whole existence which is to be understood as the "primordial sacrament," She represents the historical presence of God. Therefore, when She addresses such a word to an individual man in a critical moment in his life, and so expresses creatively the effective operation of divine grace, She utters and performs what we call a sacrament, the "irrevocable"[12] word of the grace of God, pronounced in His name, the word which not only speaks of grace but gives it a visible form in the realm of time.

The Church has seven of these sacramental formulae. One of these is the prayer of faith, accompanied by extreme unction, which is uttered over the sick man whose illness presents in a most urgent form an occasion for salvation and grace. So he invokes from the Church this word which incarnates and expresses grace in a visible form. It expresses also the need of one of Her members (or of a person presumed to be such) and effects his salvation, provided it be received with faith and the desire for forgiveness.

The prayer of faith which accompanies the anointing of the sick is the operative word of grace, which God through Christ pronounces in the Church on occasions of sickness, and it is also the voice of that silence in which a member of the Church, in mute obedience, accepts the truth of his mysterious destiny as an expression of love.

This grace which, at the moment of anointing, is promised us in the prayer of faith which the Church pronounces by the authority of Her Lord and God, is the grace which triumphs over illness, strengthens the sick and sanctifies them.

This triumph and this sanctification are necessary because of the twofold nature of the illness. But it is always one and the same grace, which may, however, according to God's will, have a two-fold aspect: it may be salvation (which includes the forgiveness of sin and release from its consequences) in the sense that the sick man recovers his bodily health and so becomes capable of continuing to live a Christian life, or it may be in the sense that he is strengthened for the last struggle and the last supreme experience of his life, and so is prepared to come face to face with death, and to die in the Lord.

The duly appointed proclaimer of this word, the dispenser of the sacrament, is the priest, because he is the "elder" who represents the Church, the holy community, the Body of Christ, and lawfully presides over the sacred feast of the assembly in which the Lord's death is proclaimed and set before us, the death which gives meaning to every other death and strength to every other life.

In order to make it more clear that the individual priest pronounces the word of faith for the healing of the sick man in the name of the whole Church, he uses for this anointing the oil which the bishop consecrates on Holy Thursday, at the beginning of the yearly commemoration of the Passion of Christ. The words which promise grace on occasions of grave illness take the form of a prayer because the way in which this grace will effectively operate is left to the merciful disposition of God.

In the normal liturgical rite not only the forehead, but all the man's senses are anointed, his eyes, ears, nose, mouth, hands, and feet, because he is totally present in these senses and through them communicates with the world and encounters its perils, and finally through them must find himself and God. In the Latin liturgy the prayer is as follows: "Through this holy anointing and through His own most tender mercy, may the Lord forgive you whatever sins you have committed through your sense of sight, your sense of hearing, your sense of smell, your sense of taste and through your ability to speak, through your sense of touch and through your ability to walk."

Naturally this prayer is accompanied by other and longer prayers which explain still more clearly the sacred meaning of the sacramental act. In the English liturgy for the sick there is also recommended a reading from Holy Scripture, the parable about the healing of the centurion's servant,[13] which is quoted as an illustration of what happens here. The accompanying prayers speak of divine blessing, of joy, of fruitful love, of everlasting salvation, of the presence of the holy angels, of the repelling of the dread Enemy. They include the repentant prayer for the forgiveness of sin, and they dare to ask for a physical recovery, for new strength and health, and that the sick man may be restored to Holy Church.

The liturgy of extreme unction is therefore not simply a liturgy for the dying but a liturgy for the sick, whose suffering is wiped away by God's grace and God's will. Of course this rite must, in normal cases, be seen together with the whole liturgy of the sick, in which the sacrament of penitence and the anointing of the sick man must lead up to the administration of the body and blood of Christ, the pledge of eternal life.

Whether we live or die we belong to the Lord. A man who is willing to belong to him in life and in death loves this earthly live and is ready for death. Both life and death may be sanctified and redeemed by the grace of God. The man who knows this has the right attitude toward sickness: he will not try to ignore the challenge which it presents.

When he is gravely ill he will, in full awareness of his

condition, frankly and bravely reply to this challenge, and this he will do also in the Sacrament of Extreme Unction.

Translated by Dorothy White

Notes

[1] James 5:14–15
[2] Cf. Acts 14:23; I Tim. 5:17; Tit. 1:5.
[3] Cf. I Tim. 4:14
[4] Mark 6:13
[5] Rom. 5:12
[6] John 9:3
[7] Cf. Peter 5:8
[8] Mark 6:13
[9] James 5:14
[10] Cf. Gen. 3:15
[11] Cf. James 5:14–16
[12] Rom. 11:29
[13] Matt. 8:5–10, 13

8

FINAL VOWS

The Eternal Yes

We are about to witness the profession of final vows, and we cannot help but note that the festive and solemn hour which we celebrate shields a content which is almost boundless. Here stands a human being who is making a decision which concerns the whole length of his life. An old and venerated abbey with a long and great history is ready to take a life thus consecrated into itself once and for all. In such a celebration the Church marks another grace-filled realization of one of the hallmarks of Her own reality. All of this points at its deepest level to God: to Him Who accepts this life, Who blesses the site of His veneration, Who makes the Church grow and Who reveals Himself in all the glory of His own life, which is eternal love.

When we truly prepare ourselves to take part in the celebration of this hour by penetrating its significance and by co-consummating it, each in his own way, all we have to do in this preparatory meditation is simply to ask: What happens here at this moment?

A human being is giving his life a definite form and direction. That is the first, the immediately tangible element here, and it is great and awesome in itself. Should one voice a hymn of praise or be silent before such daring? Should one praise

God and life, time and this hour that there are still men who have the courage to give form and configuration to their lives, the courage to want something once and forever? The courage not to be driven by the accidents of human existence, by arbitrariness and mood, by unordered shifting of their uncontrolled impulses?

Yes, to be sure, such a hymn of praise is justified. There are, we can say happily, men who see a clear configuration of life and who without fear choose in shining courage a life of dedication even though they may still fall prey to the narrowness that suffocates. There are still men who, unabashed, are sure that they can stick to a decision and carry through an all-embracing "yes," in fidelity and for a lifetime. There are still men who do not fear the finality of a simple life which has its clear place here and now, its duties and its rules. They do not consider such a life as a curse of desolate sameness, as a grinding burden of ever the same commonplaces, but as the finiteness that is the portal to infinity, as the bond that truly frees the intrinsic man.

But just when one begins to proclaim this praise of thanksgiving, one begins to be frightened. Can a man do this in this time of insecurity and anxiety? Can a man of today, hence a man who has to bear the weight of the uncertainty, the peril, the inner and outer disharmonies and the demonic urge to self-destruction of our time, the weight of skepticism and the demoralizing boredom—above all, whether or not he wants to—can such a man still praise such a static configuration of life, such silent classicalness of human existence, can he seriously take upon himself *now* something that must be fulfilled through coming decades? Does the power of such loyalty, the high-spirited courage to embrace such an eternal commitment still exist today?

Let us be honest and say simply that today there is less of this than ever before, except for the grace of God. But with God's grace it does exist. It must and it can only exist that way. Where it does exist, it is the grace of God, whether we know it or not. In order that it may exist, the grace of God is given, today as in the past, today more than in the past, because it has become more difficult. Thus it is manifest that the arm of God is not shorter or weaker, that His rule in grace and fidelity has not become more remote from us. Because His grace gives this courage, because it sustains this unprecedented risk, indeed bequeathes it, for these reasons and for these alone we can cheerfully hope that it will succeed.

But this is also the reason why the praise of such an endeavor changes into the prayer that God might shower His grace on what is vowed here, that it may consummate what it itself has begun here today. Only then does such a bond bring hope for true freedom, only then does such a commitment of life have the prospect of enduring solidity, when and because it occurs toward and from God. Such a final bond cannot occur toward an arbitrarily chosen entity. For a man's disposal over his whole life in the pure coming-together of this whole life in the inwardness of a single moment is (even if it were not expressly intended) a coming before God, unto Whom alone that is allowed and possible. Thus it is in the moment when the "yes" of everlasting love and fidelity is uttered in marriage. Thus it is today in this hour of the final and irrevocable vow.

A man gives his life to God. This is what should essentially occur in this hour.

Man as man and Christian stems from the mystery of God. God is exit and entrance, beginning and end, center and meaning. Everything belongs to Him, everything proclaims His glory, everything is subject to His grace. But man should *want* to be what he is. His life should be a single acceptance of that which he inescapably is, an answer to an almighty call. That is the task of every man, that is the expressed or secret, the accepted or denied, meaning of each life. One can say this "yes" to God, who in His mercy creates a strange and finite order to beqeath the uniqueness and infinity of His divine glory, in order to express it in a thousand forms: hidden and almost no longer conscious under the commonplaces and hardships of a life which seems to consist largely of vital self-assertion and the torment of having to die; more distinctly and somewhat more consciously expressed in the way of life that we call religion. Even the normal Christian life already has a more distinct but laboriously shielded space of its own, and one that can be combined with the thousand and more possibilities of an earthly rich and totally developed human existence full of spirit, beauty, love and fulfillment. The rare flower of God's love can bloom quietly, somehow alien and lonely, on lofty peaks or in the forgotten valleys of this earth, or it can do so magnificently, in full view of society.

But it also can be that a man and a Christian may arrive at the frightening stage where he is willing to base his whole life on this distant God, to rush toward this distant horizon of life, as if there would be nothing worth stopping for between him and this infinite distance. It is possible that a man, as if consumed by an inner fire, dares to place in the center of his tangible life that which otherwise is venerated indirectly and shyly, almost with a face turned toward the darkness or within a churchly cult whose Roman objectivity bashfully veils the ardor of the innermost heart. He dares to make the secret devotion to the formative principle of his everyday life visible to everybody, to elevate his *religio* to a vocation, to change from a man of religion into a "religious" man in order to make manifest what Christianity really is.

Is this possible? Can this be vowed? Can one organize in this way the "spirit" which, to be sure, should reign over each Christian life? Can one endow this "spirit" with such explicitness, with such tangibility? Will not man be destroyed by it? Will not the charismatic be ruined when it becomes subject to the concreteness of the institutional, the rule, the strict demands of vows, the regulations of the order and ecclesiastical precepts? These are difficult questions. Whoever answers too easily with a "yes" in favor of religious life has probably not grasped, or has tacitly devalued and cheapened, the meaning and the demands of religious life, so that he easily imagines that he can fulfill these devalued and trivialized demands and, consequently, that he can make such a vow. Nevertheless, one can and must answer "yes" to this difficult, indeed oppressive question, trusting in the grace of God. For God expects those who are called to take this risk in the name of Jesus Christ. The Gospel of Christ and the practice of the Church, indeed Her whole being, is based on the Second Coming of Christ and the transcendental kingdom of God which proclaims that there should be—and hence also can be —men who leave everything behind, who comprehend that there must be celibacy for the sake of the kingdom of heaven, whose whole existence in the Church and for the world proclaims and demonstrates that the world passes away with all its forms; that, when one rejoices, one should be as if one rejoices not, so that one mourns as though one mourns not; that the real homeland is the eternal kingdom of God and not this world, that one should let the dead bury the dead and follow Him who should be more to us than father, brother or sister.

These are hard words. But they are contained in the Gospel. The harder, the more scandalizing they sound to us, the more they incite us to overt or covert protest, the more upsetting they are for us—we who always think the Christian proves his Christianity by enthusiastically loving this world, its beauty, its tasks and its progress—the more must there be people in the Church whose lives profess for the whole Church that She is obedient to these harsh words of Her Lord. Such men, therefore, cannot have the sectarian or pharasaical pride that they alone are the real and radical Christians. Their vocation, indeed, is grace and it is only at the end of their lives that it can be determined whether they were true to it or whether this lofty vocation will signify their even deeper fall. They live therefore in fear and trembling that they, after having preached to others throughout their lives the meaning of Christianity, might themselves be condemned. In their lives, moreover, that which is hidden in every Christian life as a secret, humbly veiled essence (and often in what glory and fidelity!) must shine forth tangibly and openly: the call of grace which indeed is not of this world, but the glory of God which must be proclaimed to man beyond all human reality. And if these men in religious life, which is conceived as a vocation of a definite kind, should transform totally that which must live in each Christian heart as a pledge of the future life, which the call of God obligated them to do, then they should serve others, whom God equally loves, so that through them one should perceive what Christianity means for all: love for God from the whole heart. And then they will become frightened and mortified.

Can one see that in their lives? Are not many things which they wish to tolerate in their Christian lives too much overlaid with the normal, the bourgeois, the mediocre to which monastic life, alas, often all too surreptiously and discretely pays its tribute today? Can one see in our lives a single-mindedness where everything concerns God and no one else? Concerned with God and hence, ultimately, not with us or with our private welfare, nor with clerical-bourgeois self-assertion, nor with the power and glory of the Church, which after all must be the Church of the humble Christ, the Crucified? Is this possible? Here too our concern for the welfare of the order, the price of its Christian sublimity and dignity, turns into the contrite prayer that God may have mercy on us, so that the salt of this earth not lose its flavor, the flame on the candlestick of the Church not produce stifling smoke instead of bright light, and that the life that we lead and which is taken up today by young men in solemn vows, a life in which a man gives himself over to God, may be credible.

A man in religious life vows poverty, chastity and obedience. The means and the manner of execution for his imposed dedication of a whole life to God should lie in poverty, chastity and obedience. The formula of the Benedictine profession illustrates the content of this monastic life in a slightly different but perhaps even more striking way: *stabilitas, conversatio morum, obedientia.*

Indeed, since we must not remove ourselves to infinite distances, since the Word became flesh, then the radical, invoked and invoking expressiveness of this life cannot be kept exclusively in the secret innermost recesses of the heart. It becomes tangible and visible, hard and clear, a deed to be performed in sober everyday life. That is why the monk chooses a firm point on this earth. He settles down and vows stability, not in order to root his being into this earth, but to overcome the roving arbitrariness of mood, the egoistic self-glorification, so that the Archimedean point is achieved through which a living man obtains a location outside himself to surmount himself in God. Here I am because God places me here; here I stay so that I may not desert God. I have chosen this measurable circle because this finiteness includes the infinite God.

The monk takes the vow to observe the *conversatio morum,* the monastic way of life as it is practiced in this circle in constantly new conversion to God and His calling, so that the surrender of his being to God may be transmuted from an idea into a true reality. One can only live one's life once. And one can fail one's life. Hence one cannot experiment with this fallible life according to the promptings of one's mood or one's shortsightedness. Therefore, in the seriousness of the responsibility which knows that what is at stake is either eternal life or permanent death, the monk takes upon himself the old and wise, the tested form of life—one sanctified through generations. In its wise moderation it leaves sufficient room for the uniqueness of the individual. But, in the last analysis, this is not what concerns the monk. The new and unheard-of does not entice him. To be sure, unheard-of discoveries are still to be made in the monastic way of life. But what is, and remains, decisive for him is this: the wisdom of God, the experience of the Church and the testing through the long line of generations, which he joins as a noble man of the spirit, give him the certainty that he is not going astray when he finally takes up this way of life. And precisely because life is too serious to experiment with, because it is a one-time occurrence and even in the clearest and most classical form harbors enough dangers and sinister adventures, the monk vows to observe the prescribed form of monastic life, the *conversatio morum*, in the steadfastness of the chosen site outside himself.

But it is precisely this sanctified tradition of the established way of life which creates the holy restlessness of constant new conversion. For this way of life, by its strict injunction, sees to it that the spirit does not die, that the fire is not extinguished and that the blessed restlessness for God is not lulled to sleep, restlessness for God whom one finds only when one seeks Him, whom one loses when one thinks one has found Him forever. No order is immune to the possibility that a member may become untrue to its spirit, even though he may remain and serve it to the letter. But the experience of almost 2,000 years also shows that the *conversatio morum* that is vowed here according to the rule of Saint Benedict is a royal road along which one really can race toward the infinite spaces of God with a wide-open heart without tiring and without giving up the race before it is crowned with the laurel wreath of eternal life.

In addition to other things which are equally important, it includes poverty by which the vower renounces economic independence in favor of the community and professes a modest way of life. It also includes renunciation of the highest good of conjugal love so that the heart seeks only what is of the Lord and consumes itself freely in the praise of God and in the care for the salvation of others.

This whole way of life in the constantly renewed conversion to God, however, is formed and imprinted by the third vow which the Benedictine monk takes: obedience. By an obedience in a holy community of brotherly love and virile trusting unselfishness, by an obedience which precisely for this reason is not reified and bureaucratized because it is vowed to a man whom the vower calls "reverend father"; but also by an obedience which in its brave clarity and silent greatness ought to be the holy warrant for the fact that one does not seek oneself, that one serves others, that one surmounts oneself, so that at the end of one's life one arrives neither at the pitiable comfort of a petit-bourgeois nor does one in secret self-adulation encounter only oneself again, instead of God. The yoke of obedience is the yoke of Christ, the burden which He said is light. This obedience in a Benedictine community, despite the harshness and difficulties which He Himself may demand and which must be borne before God silently, is nevertheless wisely formed because this obedience has its measure and its form in the Rule of St. Benedict and aims to be naught else but the clarity of the Benedictine way of life which one vows in the *conversatio morum.*

All in all the *stabilitas,* the *conversatio morum,* the *obedientia* aim to be naught else but the mode and the power and the inescapable clarity with which a man bequeaths his life to God. And therefore here again we can only repeat what the abbot answers to the "volumus" of the questioned vower: *Dominus auxilietur vobis!*—may God help you! It is arduous, but it is the sober and holy arduousness of the blessedness of God.

A man consecrates himself to a monastic community and thereby to the Church and Her mission. This should not be overlooked when we speak about the significance and the importance of the celebration of this hour. Something is not only happening between God and man, but as the center and the mediator which alone vouchsafes a true immediacy, the Church is present at this hour. She becomes tangible and concrete in the hierarchically structured community of an abbey. Here the Church becomes event: in the praises of God and His mercy, in the celebration of the Passover Feast of the Lord, in the unity of love, in the common labor for the Kingdom of God, in the unity of the common bearing of Christ's cross, in the constant prayer for the departed brethren, in the mutual service which can consist in order and in obedience.

In all this the Church becomes event: for the Church is not just a world-wide organization of which the individual places and countries would be only component administrative districts. The *ecclesia* really exists in this abbey, that is to say, here the Church Herself becomes event, for here the highest mystery is being celebrated, which is not only fixed by people of the Church through orders of the whole Church but in which precisely this Church finds Her highest realization. And around this mystery in which the Church Herself executes Her deepest being in the most real and innermost way, She builds everything else pertaining to a monastic community, so that the Church can be represented and realized there, so that the Church is here and now in this community.

When a man therefore bequeaths and consecrates himself and his whole life through such a *militia Christi* to such a monastery-church, it has to do with the Church of Christ not only insofar as She accepts such vows, supervises their fulfillment, and guides and preserves through Her legislation the life of the order growing from it. Neither is it only a matter of the Church recognizing such life as an expression of Her own spirit and the holy fruit of Her pastoral endeavor to effect the Christianization of mankind. Such a profession and monastic vow is an act of the Church, here on this site itself, and thereby an act of the Church in general. The Church not only supports this event approvingly and protectingly, but She Herself becomes an event in it. What happens here is the lofty act of faith, of hope in eternity, of love of God and the brotherly community.

But when one asks: where then is the Church, where does the Church become event, a holy convocation of people to divine grace, which redeems and blesses with God Himself, and to the fellowship of men in God? In the ultimate and truest sense we need not answer: where laws are enacted and

Church policy (as important and divinely willed as that may also be) is made. Instead, we must say: there where faith, hope and love happen, there where life is consecrated to the accomplishment of the eternal Eucharist and is dedicated to the eternal God. Therein does the Church become event. Therefore the Church grows in this hour, therefore does She, in such an event, appear in Her truest essence, which is the apportionment of the world which God Himself brings tangibly into being through His grace in the freedom of the infinite Spirit.

All that we celebrate here is only a beginning, a vow, not yet the accomplishment, the fulfillment. Such a beginning and such a vow are difficult. Even more difficult, however, are the accomplishment and the fulfillment. They are effected throughout a lifetime, a long life full of work, full of disappointment in oneself, in everything which is not God Himself, Whom we repeatedly take for someone else and thus think that we have been disappointed by Him. Therefore such a beginning rooted in a vow leads into the unknown, unforeseeable and really is a risk.

Man is not master of his ways, not even when he goes the royal way of Christ in the community of true brothers. God alone is master of these ways, through His unfathomable guidance, through His dark and shining grace in the inner man. Therefore when a man takes leave as on this day, the prayers of our hearts must accompany him: *Dominus auxilietur vobis!* May the Lord go with you, may the Lord be with you! All ways lead into His infinity when He shows the way, when He goes with you, when He is the way, and the power to walk along this way.

All ways—the streets of labor for the Kingdom of God, the quiet paths of holy contemplation, the stations of the cross— all lead toward death, all lead to God. What is being vowed today is like a compass for these ways and for the vows: one can really walk along them until they end in the infinity and freedom of God. May God be with you on these ways. He is a true God. He will not tempt you beyond that which you can bear. He triumphs in your weakness; and on the day of Jesus Christ He will consummate the work that He has begun in you today.   Amen.

Translated by Salvator Attanasio